Scrapbooks & **BEYOND**

OVER 150 INNOVATIVE
DESIGNS AND TECHNIQUES
FROM THE TALENTED ARTISTS AT
STAMPER'S WAREHOUSE

KOOLER DESIGN STUDIO BOOKS

PRODUCED BY

Kooler Design Studio, Inc. • 399 Taylor Blvd., Ste. 104
  Pleasant Hill, CA 94523 • kds@koolerdesign.com
  www.koolerdesign.com
Creative Director, Donna Kooler
Project Manager, Book Designer, Photo Stylist, Basha Kooler Hanner
Writers, Basha Kooler Hanner, Kit Schlich, Project Designers
Editor/Production, Judy Swager
Proofreader, Chris Mitchell, Marsha Hinkson
Photographer, Dianne Woods

10 9 8 7 6 5 4 3 2 1

Library of Congress Cataloging-in-Publication Data
    Kooler, Donna
    Scrapbooks & Beyond
    "A Leisure Arts Publication"

I S B N :   1 - 5 7 4 8 6 - 4 3 5 - 1

PUBLISHED BY
LEISURE ARTS
the art of everyday living

PRINTED WITH SOY INK

Made in U.S.A.

COVER PROJECTS: Barbara De Lap,
Linda Lavasani, Vanessa Cole

Welcome

to the world of Stamper's Warehouse where the lines are blurred, borders crossed and anything goes. Papercraft melds with assemblage, collage, bookmaking and more. Read on to be inspired…

PROJECT DESIGNERS

Sandi Allan

Sue Astroth

Traci Bautista

Krista Camacho

Patty Carlson

Vanessa Cole

Debby DeBenedetti

Barbara De Lap

Diana Diaz

Jennifer Gaub

Linda Lavasani

Sandi Marr

Phyllis Nelson

Janis Ramsden

Terrece Siddoway

Kathy Yee

WITH ADDITIONAL PROJECTS BY:
Lari Drendall, Emily Foytlin,
Susan Gin, Jaye Green,
DeAnne Velasco Musiel,
April Nelson, Margaret Rodgers,
and Marian Wilde

Contents

What's in Store

FROM THE MOMENT THE DOORS OPEN UNTIL THE LATE hours of a Friday evening "crop night," a creative buzz hovers in the air at Stamper's Warehouse, a small storefront tucked away in historic Danville, California. This excitement originates with the cast and crew who make up the core of designers who work, teach, and hang out at Stamper's Warehouse. Led by owner Phyllis Nelson, manager Terrece Siddoway, and Phyllis' daughter April Nelson, the store is a bustle of activity and inspiration. From the intriguing merchandise in the store front to the well-used classroom in back, the atmosphere is more than just a store: it's a community meeting place, a family affair like the quilting bees of yore. Three entwined elements comprise the secret to the success of Stamper's Warehouse: a fabulous inventory, a lively class schedule, and a dedicated staff.

Phyllis' retailing adventure can be called a true grass roots enterprise. A former preschool teacher with no formal art training, she discovered rubber stamping as a hobby in 1979 when her children were young, and sold stamps at boutiques. She began selling stamping supplies out of her garage at once-a-month events, and built up a mailing list. When stamping grew in popularity and the first stores exclusively devoted to stamping appeared in the late 80s, Phyllis was on the ground floor, and her business grew.

The original retail space was once occupied by a cookie store; the landlord "wasn't impressed" with Phyllis' proposed business and was skeptical that a

stamping store could be successful. But Stamper's Warehouse thrived and became the destination shop in the center. Expansion was inevitable: ten years later, the current Danville shop is the third location, boasting 22 employees.

Stamper's Warehouse draws enthusiasts from afar, not just from the San Francisco Bay Area and northern California. Out-of-state vacationers find their way to Danville, lured by the store's reputation. Keeping the inventory vital and interesting is a pleasure for the store staff. "We get to be the 'ultimate consumers,'" Phyllis says with satisfaction. "We keep our merchandise fresh, and new merchandise arrives every day!"

As enthusiasm for scrapbooking emerged in the mid '90s the creative minds at Stamper's Warehouse realized that it dovetailed nicely with stamping. Merging the two techniques engendered cross-pollination: stampers found scrapbooks the ideal medium to display their technique; scrapbookers loved the effects that stamping imparts to pages. This "marriage" has spawned new offspring such as bookbinding, altered art, and just about any sort of decorative expression that one can apply to the blank page. In much the same way that quilters fall in love with fabrics and needleworkers adore new threads, scrapbookers appreciate fine paper. Merely viewing a collection of quality paper products is enough to stimulate artistic urges.

All members of the artistic community flock to Stamper's Warehouse for supplies and inspiration. Students are drawn to the store's inventory and find what they need for creative school projects.

Phyllis and her staff are responsive to their customers needs. Once shoppers have sampled and mastered a particular technique, they're driven to continually explore new, related techniques to build on and expand their artistic skills. While understanding this craving is useful, knowing how to satisfy it is priceless. To this end, Phyllis and her staff have devised a dizzying array of classes to keep the clientele satisfied "beyond stamping and scrapbooking." Classes include how to make paper, enhance photography, create books and journals, jewelry, and decorative art of all kinds, as well as how to use the ever-expanding array of new products. Stamper's Warehouse offers classes which are taught by many of the artists featured in this book and by nationally known guest instructors.

In her years as a stamper, scrapbooker and retailer, Phyllis has watched her favorite "craft" emerge as true graphic art, claiming its place beside fine art as a worthwhile creative endeavor. She is especially pleased that it draws many

individuals who do not consider themselves "artists," but nevertheless possess artistic sensibilities and skills which emerge with a little encouragement. And that's exactly what the staff at Stamper's Warehouse loves to do. Phyllis' professional mission is to keep her customers creatively inspired.

This book, *Scrapbooks & Beyond*, gathers designers affiliated with Stamper's Warehouse and showcases their creations. Their concepts will inspire you to think "outside the book" and see beyond scrapbooking. May you delight in original bookbinding, card making, jewelry, and three-dimensional projects to take you on new paths of discovery.

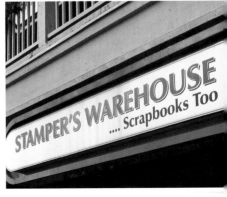

Materials

THE JOY OF PAPER

A blank sheet of paper—and all its infinite possibilities—is the starting point for your creativity. As you embrace the possibilities and face the fear of jumping into an unknown direction to capture a moment in time, your chosen paper will form the foundation of your vision.

To realize your creative dreams, there's no substitute for a trip to your local craft shop for inspiration and the joy of visual and tactile stimulation. The variety of colors, textures, and weights are impressive, so carefully consider the role each paper will play in your envisioned project.

CHOOSING PAPER

Cardstock is the best choice for scrapbook pages, and it should be heavy enough to support multiple added layers. It also works well for decorative cutouts such as journaling boxes, tags, and photo mats. Vellum adds a sheer, luxurious layer of decorative accent to background paper. Handmade papers, whether purchased or made at home, add interesting textures and come in a variety of weights for memory pages or original bookmaking. Rice, mulberry, and Washi papers make wonderful accents in a rainbow of colors and weights; the tissue-weight is especially useful for special effects. Specialty papers such as wrapping paper offer a new dimension of decorative patterns. Choose acid-free papers to protect your images or memorabilia.

USING PAPER

One of the most dramatic effects in paper craft is created by building layers of paper to highlight and frame your chosen images. Experiment with complementary and contrasting colors, weights, and textures, and try varying the layers with straight-cut, specialty-cut, and torn edges.

When designing cards, size them to fit standard envelopes, unless you also plan to make the envelopes.

An endless variety of cardstock is only the beginning of an original creation.

ADHESIVES

There are many options for connecting elements. Choosing the best adhesive to attach embellishments will guarantee the life of projects for generations to come. Some adhesives not only attach the item, but add a decorative touch as well.

Mono Multi glue by Tombow, and two-way glue pens are great for standard bonding. They work well on small areas and are also acid-free. A roll-up glue stick is a good choice when a quick application is needed to bond paper to paper. Tacky glues including Aleene's Tacky and The Ultimate and Incredible Tacky glue by Crafter's Pick are excellent glues when a stronger bond is required. Different brands work best with different materials, so it is wise to read the labels for the manufacturer's recommendations. E6000 provides extra hold and dries clear. PVA bookbinder's adhesive is intended for book-making projects. Gel mediums are also used in projects to adhere dimensional items to an artist's work. Mod Podge and Liquid Laminate are thin wet glues for decoupage applications.

Several products on the market are glass-like glues that double as an accent medium with a clear dimensional effect. They include JudiKin's Diamond Glaze, Sakura's Crystal Lacquer, and Ranger's Crystal Accents. They vary in viscosity but the results are similar.

Double-sided adhesive tapes and sheets are versatile craft products. Different brands vary in strength. They are flexible and will stick to surfaces that other products resist. The sheets and tape are often used to bond beads, glitter and metal foils. Decorative pieces can be cut from the sheets; tapes can be used for embossing borders.

Glue Dots in various sizes offer an instant and sturdy way to attach embellishments. The Pop-Up Glue Dots and foam mounting tape not only bond but also create dimension.

Xyron machines now come in many sizes. Depending on the cartridge used, they are versatile tools used to laminate, or to apply a magnetic surface or adhesive to paper.

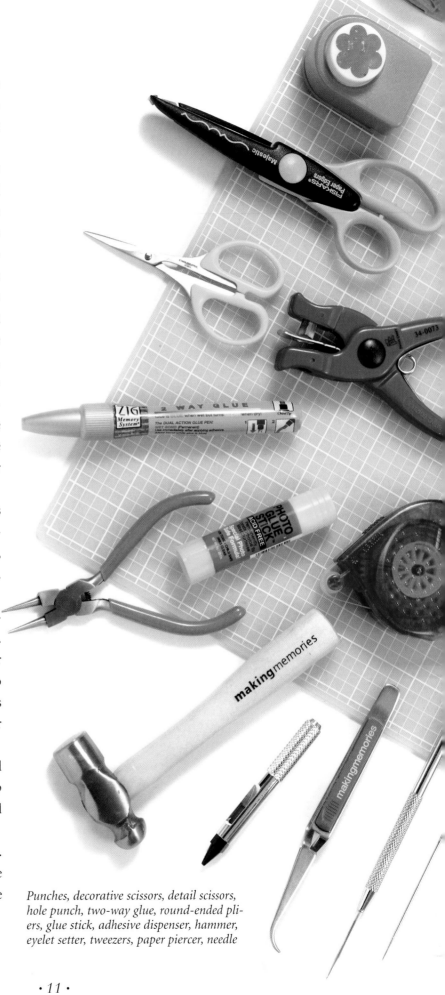

Punches, decorative scissors, detail scissors, hole punch, two-way glue, round-ended pliers, glue stick, adhesive dispenser, hammer, eyelet setter, tweezers, paper piercer, needle

WRITING INSTRUMENTS

The pen market seems to have exploded with an almost overwhelming assortment of colors and types of pens. They are great tools for labeling and journaling, as well as for creating decorative effects. There are new varieties of gel pens as well as watercolor markers with an assortment of tip shapes and sizes. Colored pencils layer color and provide a colored accent to papers of all shades and tones. Watercolor pencils produce wonderfully soft effects. Blending pens for watercolor markers and colored pencils are available from several companies. Chartpak's xylene-based blender is often used to transfer images to paper and polymer clay. Chalks, applied with sponges or cotton swabs, provide color, soften edges and add dimensionality. Krylon's metallic leafing pens in gold silver and copper are indispensable for applying a straight border around a paper edge.

TOOLS

The right tool for the job makes any project easier. Scrapbookers will find the following tools especially useful.

- Scissors, including specialty scissors with decorative edges
- Craft knife and self-healing mat
- Paper cutter or trimmer
- Circle cutters
- Cutting systems and templates
- Cutting mats
- Punches
- Rulers — clear and cork-backed
- Bone folders
- Stylus
- Tweezers
- "Anywhere" hole punches, eyelet setter, and hammer
- Awl (also called paper piercer)
- Needles
- Heat tool
- Glue gun

Frames, stickers, photo corners, letter stickers, inkpad, stamps, embossing pad, embossing powder, pressed flowers, pens

YOUR PERSONAL STAMP

STAMPS AND STAMPING MATERIALS

Most of the designers who contributed to this book began their artistic endeavors using rubber stamps. This exciting medium has grown in recent years, as manufacturers and designers introduce new materials and techniques. Stamping with inkpads alone or with heat embossing effects is a versatile technique of paper embellishment. Embossing powders offer an array of raised effects. Try a variety of powders to give raised, textured or pearlized accents to stamped images. Add gold leafing and stickers of all sorts for lively design accents and borders.

DIMENSIONAL PAGE EMBELLISHMENTS

Adding dimensional accents to pages can take an artist in any direction and a glance at this book's table of contents offers a hint of what's possible. Anything goes these days, blurring the line between paper craft and mixed media collage. Purchased embellishments and notions of all kinds (charms, beads, buttons, wire, tags, fabrics, ribbons, flowers, leaves, lace, and fibers) add a tactile effect. Personal mementos can be souvenirs, jewelry, feathers, shells, flea market treasures, even collected "junk" such as watch parts and game pieces. These items often give personal meaning to your creations.

JOURNALING

Along with photographs, your own words are the most personal touch you add to your pages. Words add meaning and context for the images and leave a message for those who will receive or inherit your work. Choose a lettering style — bold block letters, fanciful script, or a specialty font — that complements your images and message. For titles or text, use pens, stamps, colored pencils, templates, paper cut outs, rub-on alphabets, and computer printouts of decorative fonts. Be sure to use acid-free photosafe, archival products.

This book will help bring out the artist and graphic designer in you. Be inspired and enjoy!

Wire, letter tiles, seed packet, charms, frames, ribbon, fibers, miscellaneous ephemera, compass, eyelets, dog tags, feathers, buttons, beads

Bookbinding

Creative bookmaking takes you far beyond scrapbooking. Here are some strikingly original ideas for binding books: using beads, barbecue skewers, leather with braiding, fantasy fibers, and unusual hinges, as well as a handy wallet-style binding.

PIANO HINGE BOOK
By Barbara De Lap

13 wooden skewers
2 pieces heavy textured cardstock
   5^1/$_2$" x 8^1/$_2$"
24 pieces cardstock 5^1/$_2$"x 8^1/$_2$"
4-ply waxed linen thread
Charms
PVA glue

Directions: Fold each piece of textured cardstock in half. Glue the insides of the folded piece leaving a space of ^{1}/$_2$" from the folded side of the spine unglued so that the skewers can slide through. Cut pieces out of the covers to accommodate signatures. Front Cover: from the top of the spine measure down 1" and cut out a piece that is 1^1/$_8$" long and ^{1}/$_2$" deep. Measure down 1^1/$_8$" to make the next cut 1^1/$_8$" by ^{1}/$_2$" . All spine cuts are the same size. Back Cover: at the top of the spine you will cut out a piece that is 1^1/$_8$" long, ^{1}/$_2$" deep. Measure down 1^1/$_8$", then cut out another identically sized piece. The third identical cut is made 1^1/$_8$" piece. Fold the 24 pieces of cardstock in half to 5^1/$_2$" x 4^1/$_2$". Nestle and place together two of these papers to make a signature. Mark and cut out four ^{1}/$_4$" triangular shaped notches on each signature. These notches should correspond to the top and bottom of cutouts on the book cover. The first notch starts 1^1/$_8$" down from top of signature and measures ^{1}/$_4$" tapering to a point toward the inside of the signature. Assemble the book using the piano hinge technique. When assembled, trim skewers. Weave the waxed linen thread around the skewers at the top and bottom. Use PVA glue to "set" the thread into place. Trim the thread at the bottom, but at the top leave enough thread to make braids for dangling charms.

BRAIDED LEATHER BOOK
By Barbara De Lap

2 pieces book board 8^3/$_4$" x 5^3/$_4$ "
1 piece book board 8^3/$_4$" x 1^1/$_2$"
1 piece garment-weight leather
   14^1/$_2$" x 10^3/$_4$"
1 piece book cloth 13" x 8^1/$_2$"
60 sheets text-weight paper 8^1/$_2$" x 11"
4-ply waxed linen thread
PVA glue
Japanese screw punch
Tapestry needle
Cutting mat

Directions: On the work surface, place the two large pieces of book board for the covers with the narrow piece in the center. The pieces should be spaced ^{3}/$_{16}$" apart. Glue the leather to the book board. Turn the piece over and glue the book cloth to the reverse side of the book board. This will be the inside of the cover. Using the screw punch, make small holes in spine. There will be a total of ten holes down the spine and six holes across the width for a total of 60 holes. Placement from the top of the spine to the first hole measures down ^{11}/$_{16}$". Proceed measuring down for consecutive holes as follows: ^{5}/$_8$", ^{3}/$_8$", ^{1}/$_2$", ^{3}/$_8$", 1^3/$_4$", ^{3}/$_8$", ^{1}/$_2$", ^{3}/$_8$", and 1^5/$_8$" for the last hole. For the spacing between the sets of holes, measure ^{3}/$_{16}$" between each set (see photo). Fold each sheet of text weight paper in half. Nestle ten pieces of paper together to make a signature. Punch holes in the signatures to match the holes along the length of the book spine. Sew together using the braided bookbinding technique that can be found in the book *Non-Adhesive Binding* by Keith Smith.

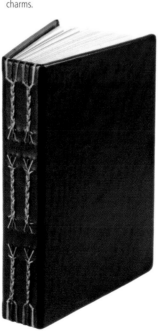

BEADED BINDING
By Barbara De Lap

2 pieces book board 8^3/$_4$" x 5^3/$_4$"
2 sheets decorative paper 8^1/$_2$" x 11"
2 pieces cardstock 8^1/$_2$" x 5"
32 sheets text weight paper 8^1/$_2$" x 11"
Three 9" lengths of 1" wide grosgrain ribbon
Thirty 4 mm. square glass beads
PVA glue
4-ply waxed linen thread
Tapestry needle
Awl & cutting mat

Directions: Cover each piece of book board with the decorative paper using the PVA glue and let dry. Fold each sheet of text weight paper in half. Nestle four pieces of paper together to make a signature. Punch eight holes in the signatures. From the top measure down ^{1}/$_2$" for the first hole, ^{7}/$_8$", then 1", 1^5/$_{16}$", 1, 1^5/$_{16}$", 1", and ^{7}/$_8$" for the last hole. Sew the signatures together using the "sewn over tape" style of bookbinding. The beads are sewn over the ribbon pieces on the third and sixth signatures, forming the spine. Using the PVA glue, attach the ribbon onto the front and back cover. Keep the ribbon flat and the covers tight to the signatures. Glue the cardstock over the ribbon to hold it in place. This is the end sheet of the book. Place a heavy weight on the book while it dries.

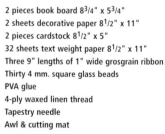

SOUTHWEST JOURNAL
By Terrece Siddoway

2 pieces black book board
Text-weight paper sized slightly smaller than book board
Dye-based inkpads
Colored pencils
Assorted western stamps
Old West images from books & magazines
Fibers, beads, charms
4-ply waxed linen thread
Japanese screw punch
Awl & cutting mat
Liquid Applique – brown, black, gold, white
Brayer
Eyelets & eyelet tools

Directions: This book contains images and scenes from the Old West. Use colored pencils to add color to the images which have been stamped on the pages. Singe page edges or rub with a brown inkpad to create a weathered look. Add texture to the black book board covers using a faux leather technique. To create the faux leather, squirt black, brown, gold, and white liquid applique colors on a piece of waxed paper. Roll a brayer through the colors then apply to covers. Continue this application until the board is completely covered with a fairly thin layer. Once covered, heat the entire area with a heat gun. The applique will puff and the color will soften creating the uneven look and feel of distressed leather. Fold the text-weight papers and nestle even groups together for the signatures. Punch four holes in spine edge of each cover, spacing them evenly (see photo). Fasten eyelets in holes. Pierce holes in signatures to match eyelets and lace with waxed linen thread. Tie off and add fibers with a fountain of beads and charms.

DREAM JOURNAL
By Emily Foytlin

2 pieces of wood 7" x 8" x $1/4$"
2 pieces of wood $1^1/2$" x 8" x $1/4$"
Hinges
2 screwposts
Rusting agent
Various rubber stamps
Inkpads
Fibers
Charms & found metal pieces
Handmade papers & text weight papers
Spray paint & sealer
Button & fiber for clasp

Directions: Cut $1/4$" thick wood to size as listed and sand smooth. Spray paint the wood. Pre-drill the holes for the screwposts and the hinges in the narrow wood for the spine pieces. Attach the larger cover pieces with aged metal hinges. Stamp cover and back as desired. Add found objects and charms for embellishments. Spray with clear sealer. Add paper for inside pages with holes matching screw posts and assemble. Attach button and fiber for clasp closure.

AGING METAL: This technique can be used to add rust and antique finish to most metals (not suitable for brass). Put rusting agent or acetone in a glass bowl. Completely immerse metal in solvent and let sit until corrosion occurs. Allow to dry on a paper towel and coat with clear sealant.

WRAPPED & TIED
By Barbara De Lap

Embossed leather 13" x $4^3/4$"
30 pieces of text weight paper $4^1/2$" x 8"
4-ply waxed linen thread
Paper piercer
Awl & cutting mat

Directions: Cut the leather so the right-hand flap edge has a curve to it (see photo). Measure $4^3/4$" from the square end and fold over to mark the spine. Punch five holes along this fold line. The first hole should be placed $5/8$" down from the top edge; then $1/2$" down for hole 2, 1" down for hole 3, 1" down for hole 4, and $1/2$" down for hole 5. Fold the text weight paper in half. Nestle ten pieces of paper together to form a signature. You will have three signatures for this book. Punch holes in the signatures that match the holes in the leather spine area. Sew the book together using the crossed-spine binding as seen in Keith Smith's book *Non Adhesive Binding*. Punch three holes in the curved part of the leather. Loop waxed linen thread through these holes. Braid threads long enough to wrap around the book and knot the end.

Book Covers

What makes a stronger statement than your own cover design for a book or journal? These distinctively different and dramatic covers use materials as simple as paper or as innovative as game boards to inspire your own personal expression.

DOUBLE DUTY JOURNAL
By Barbara De Lap

1 piece book board 11" x 8^1/$_2$"
2 pieces book board 8^1/$_2$" x 5^1/$_2$"
96 sheets text weight paper 8^1/$_2$" x 11"
1 piece decorative paper 12" x 10^1/$_2$"
2 pieces decorative paper 10^3/$_4$" x 8^1/$_4$"
1 sheet cardstock weight paper 8^1/$_2$" x 11"
2 pieces cardstock weight paper 8^1/$_2$" x 5^1/$_4$"
4-ply waxed linen thread
Tapestry needle
Japanese screw punch & cutting mat
Eyelets & eyelet tools
PVA glue

Directions: Cover the large piece of book board with decorative paper, using PVA glue. Glue cardstock to the opposite side. Cover the smaller pieces of book board in the same manner. Punch six holes on the sides of each of the three cover pieces of book board (see photo for placement). Measure down ^{1}/$_2$" for hole 1; 1^1/$_4$" for hole 2; 1^5/$_8$" for hole 3; 2^1/$_8$" for hole 4; 1^3/$_8$" for hole 5; and 1^1/$_8$" for hole 6. Place these holes on the left side of the left front cover and on the right side of the right front cover. Place the same holes on the back cover. Fold the text weight paper in half. Nestle four pieces of paper together to form one signature for a total of 24 signatures. Punch holes in the signatures to match the holes made in the book board. Place 12 of the signatures on one side of the book. Bind the book using waxed linen thread and the Coptic style of bookbinding found in *Non-Adhesive Binding* by Keith Smith. Repeat this method for the other side of the book.

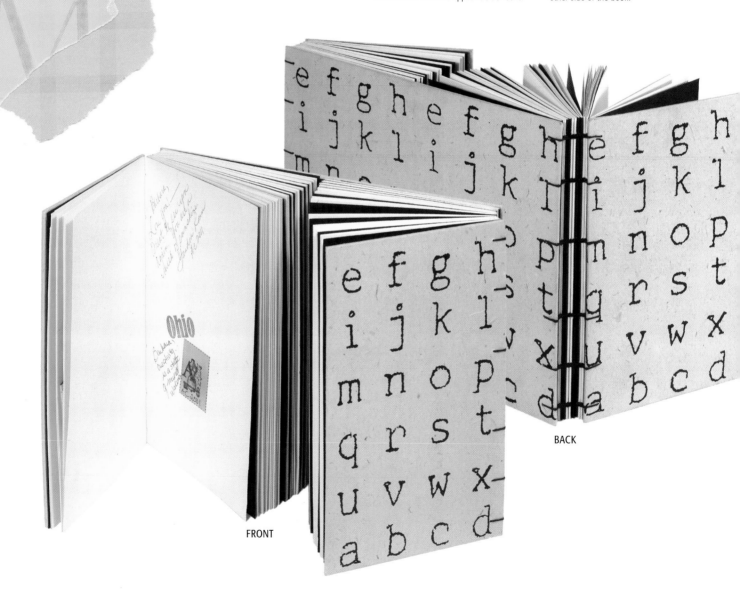

FRONT

BACK

GAMES FROM YOUR PAST
By Barbara De Lap

Old game board
32 pieces text weight paper (cut to size
    depending upon the game board size)
4-ply waxed linen thread
Tapestry needle
Japanese screw punch & cutting mat
Eyelets & eyelet tools
Color copies of game board

Directions: Before cutting the game board, make color copies of it to use as signature wraps for the first and last signature in the book. Cut the game board to the desired size. To get two books from one board, cut it in half at the original fold in the board, then cut each resulting piece in half. Using the Japanese screw punch, punch four evenly spaced holes into the game board. Fasten eyelets into the holes using an eyelet setter. Fold your text weight paper in half so that it will fit the cut game board. Use the holes placed in the front and back cover as your guide for punching the holes into your text weight paper signatures. Nestle four pieces of paper together to create a signature. Assemble eight signatures. Bind the book together using waxed linen thread and the Coptic style of bookbinding found in *Non-Adhesive Binding* by Keith Smith.

PRIORITY PURSE
By Patty Carlson

U.S. Post Office Priority mailing box
Duct tape
3 wooden beads with large hole for cord
Velcro tabs
18"–36" cord (for purse handle)
Liquid Laminate by Beacon
Single-fold bias tape
Large piece Japanese Washi paper & 6–10
    pieces of Washi paper in coordinating
    colors
Piercing tool

Directions: Line the inside of the box with Washi paper, adhering with glue. Assemble the box, using duct tape on the outside edges to add stability. Cut assorted Washi papers into about 140 small triangles and glue to the outside of the box, covering it in a random fashion. When dry, apply several coats of Liquid Laminate with a brush, allowing to dry between coats. Measure the edges of the lid and purse opening. Cut bias tape slightly longer than the measured length. Apply to the edge with white craft glue, stretching the bias tape as you go. Using a piercing tool, make two holes 2" from each edge at the top of the flap. Enlarge the holes from the outside enough to accommodate the cording. String the wrapped beads on the cord and thread the cord through the holes. Tie knots on both ends (inside the purse). Seal knots and cord ends with Liquid Laminate. Place Velcro tabs on inside of flap and front of box.

GARDEN DIARY
By Sue Astroth

1 sheet leaf print cardstock 8 1/2" x 11"
5 sheets cream cardstock 8 1/2" x 11"
Green pens & inkpads
1 bamboo reed
1 yard sheer green ribbon
1 scrap each cream & green cardstock
Alphabet, assorted leaf, & bird stamps
Japanese screw punch & cutting mat
Deckle edge ruler

Directions: Cut leaf print cardstock in half. With deckle edge ruler placed in center of sheet of cream cardstock, tear five pieces of cream cardstock in half and stamp with various combinations of bird and leaf stamps in two shades of green ink. Stamp "Garden Diary" title on scrap of cream cardstock; cut out and layer with scrap of green. Machine sew label to front cover following the photo for placement. Stack the cover and pages together. Make 1/8" holes 1/2" in from the edge of the cover pieces in three places: 1" from the top and bottom and one in the center. Lay reed on the top of front cover. Wrap ribbon around the reed, through the book holes and finish off bows.

WRAPPED BEADS: Cut a piece of Washi paper to fit around a small wooden bead. Fold paper in half lengthwise. From the unfolded edge, cut slashes into the edge but not to the fold. Unfold and brush white glue on the wrong side of the paper. Adhere paper to the bead, smoothing as you go. Apply Liquid Laminate to the finished beads.

Modifying Books

There are already so many appealing blank books available for art journaling… why not simply modify an existing book to your personal style? As you can see, these covers are bursting with inspiration, inviting you to look inside.

HOME BOOK
By Sandi Allan

Purchased album
Patterned cardstock
Colored cardstock to fit album cover
Computer printed title on colored paper
Oval & lettering stickers
Glue
Fibers
Daisy punch

Directions: Attach colored cardstock to front and back of album. Glue patterned paper to colored cardstock on front. Adhere title strip on top. Center oval sticker on patterned paper and add "HOME" lettering stickers on top. For inside pages, mat photos on patterned paper. Glue computer-printed title strip on colored paper and adhere at top of page. Embellish each end of title with daisy flower punch. Color center of each daisy with gel pen. Punch two small holes near center of small paper strip, thread fiber through and knot. Make tag from patterned paper. Mat the date piece and attach. Punch hole near top of tag. Thread fiber through it and knot. Glue tag and small strip to pages as shown.

JUST US
By Vanessa Cole

Purchased journal
Blue jeans paper
Coil by 7 Gypsies
Elastic cord by 7 Gypsies
Eyelets & eyelet tools
Blue cardstock

Directions: Apply jeans paper to cover front and back of small square spiral-bound book. Attach metal coil to elastic cord and position it around the front cover. Cut out tags from blue paper. Add lettering for title. Center an eyelet at the top of each tag using an eyelet setter. Attach tags to coil.

ANNIVERSARY BOOK
By Vanessa Cole

Blank journal
Papers by Personal Stamp Exchange
Sticker letters by Creative Imaginations,
    Provo Craft, & Pebbles
Sticker words by Pebbles
Heart eyelets & eyelet tools
Formica sample tile
Legal envelopes cut in half
Embellishments & memorabilia
Fibers & ribbon

Directions: Layer papers on journal pages and adhere. Attach envelope half as a pocket. Make tags using cardstock. Add sticker letters and words, then attach heart-shaped eyelets. Embellish Formica tile with various words and letters. Attach memorabilia with fibers and ribbons to finish.

GARDEN OF DAYLILIES
By Margaret Rodgers

Purchased journal
Photos
Leaf punch
Skeleton leaf
PVA glue
Glazes by Golden
Stamp for text
Decorative corner punch

Directions: This was designed as a remembrance of Margaret's mother-in-law who grew over 600 daylilies and kept notes about them in her journal. Start by printing the garden background on a transparency. It is easiest to position this on the journal pages by using a Xyron machine with an adhesive cartridge. Leave two blank pages in the middle of the transparency layout. Simultaneously tear these pages randomly. Paint the front and back of the torn pages with glaze. Punch through both pages to create a window. Tape a skeleton leaf between the pages to cover the punched leaf shape. Glue the two pages together with PVA. Punch the corners of the computer-printed photo with a decorative corner punch. Add the text at the top with a rubber stamp.

Designer Originals

The designers at Stamper's Warehouse pull out all the stops to dazzle you with creative original books and projects full of clever embellishment. The surprise pockets and tags ensure an interactive trip through the pages for the viewer.

HALLOWEEN BOOK
By Vanessa Cole

6 pieces black cardstock 6" x 12"
6 pieces orange cardstock 5^1/$_2$" x 12"
6 pieces purple cardstock 5^1/$_4$" x 12"
6 pieces handmade paper or vellum 6^1/$_2$"x 11"
6 wooden skewers 6" long
Ribbon, yarn, & fibers
Charms & beads
Metal letter charms
Sticker letters
Tags
Halloween die cuts
Mini eyelets & eyelet tools
Assorted stamps & stickers
Paper piercing tool
Blunt needle

Directions: Fold all of the papers in half. Stack six sets of four each in the following order: black, orange, purple, vellum. Turn two stacks over to the reverse. Use the paper piercing tool to make a hole 1" from the top and bottom of each stack. This will be the first and last sets in the book stack. In the remaining four sets of papers (middle sets), make four holes 1" apart starting from the top on each set of papers. Stack papers so that the sets with two holes are at the front and back of the stack. Bind the book using a blunt needle and fiber. Cut the fiber into twelve 7" strips. Threading from the outside, take 7" fiber and go through set 1, top hole. Wrap around skewer and bring it back out the same hole. Take the other end of the fiber and put it into the top hole of set 2. Wrap around skewer and bring back out. Do the same with both sets at the bottom holes and tie the ends of the fibers together. Add the third set. Bind sets 2 and 3 together using the middle holes, working as you did for the first sets and tying off each time. Alternate holes for each set and bind off set 6 using top and bottom holes. Add charms to fiber ends. Decorate book using tags, letters, die cuts, and eyelets.

NICK BANTOCK POCKET
By Vanessa Cole

Leather-textured paper
Eyelets & eyelet tools
Nick Bantock collage images & postcards
Nick Bantock inkpads
Collage rubber stamps
Laminate material
Ball chain
Metal tags
Brayer

Directions: Construct a pocket holder from brown leather paper. Add collage images to the front cover. Cut several cards to fit the pocket and brayer them using a variety of dye inks. Stamp images in black ink on the backs of the cards . Glue the postcards cut to fit. All the cards should be laminated and holes punched in one corner. Use a ball type chain to attach the cards to the pocket and slip inside. Decorate the chain with tags.

A LIFETIME OF MEMORIES
By Traci Bautista

Assorted cardstock, printed papers, textured
    paper & vellum
Foam core, 5"X 5"
Manila tags & vellum envelopes
Eyelets & eyelet tools
Metal foil in copper tone & stylus
Mini quilting iron by Clover
Brown crayons & metallic glitter
Pigment inkpads
Wonder tape sheet
Glass micro beads
Lightning Black Brilliance inkpad
Stamps: alphabet letters & decorative
    images
Text-weight paper & transparencies printed
    with images & text by inkjet printer

Metallic Rub-Ons
Colorless blender by Chartpak
Make-up sponge
Acrylic paints by Golden
Lumiere, Neopaque & textile paints by
    Jacquard
Gel medium, matte or glossy by Golden
Collage images & items such as beads,
    fibers, fabric scraps, lace, ribbons, but-
    tons, silk flowers & family mementos
Color copies of family photos

Directions: For the cover, wrap foam core
with textured paper. Adhere photo. Emboss
title on metal foil; adhere to cover with double-sided tape. Embellish with collage
images and items, using gel medium to
adhere. Create an accordion book structure.
Use bone folder to crease paper. Create
pocket pages by gluing two (9" x 12")
pieces of printed paper back-to-back and
folding to 6" x 12", then fold in half with
pockets facing outward. Fold 6" x 12" cardstock pages in half to 6" x 6". Attach folded pages to spine with glue or eyelets.

    Create a decorative medallion with melt-
ed crayon. Preheat craft iron, protecting
work surface with aluminum foil. Melt
crayons into a small puddle with iron. Press
a rubber stamp on the pigment inkpad and
then immediately press it in the crayon puddle. Highlight with metallic Rub-Ons.

    Glue photo to a tag. Add sheet of
Wonder tape on top of photo; cut to size.
Remove remaining release sheet and cover
with glass micro beads. Press beads firmly
onto adhesive sheets with fingers. Edge
with Lightning Black inkpad. Transfer images
and words on pages with blender pen.
Burnish images with bone folder. Rub on
pigments inks with a make-up sponge. Use
fibers or ribbons for tag strings. Decorate
pages, vellum envelopes and additional tags
with stamped images, pigment inks and
paints. Place family mementos in envelopes.
Insert embellished tags, photos and
envelopes in page pockets.

ACCORDION ENVELOPE BOOK
By Sandi Marr

1 sheet brown leather-textured paper,
    8^1/$_2$" X 11" for covers
1 sheet black text paper 8^1/$_2$" X 11"
6 coin envelopes
6 manila tags
Stamps: alphabet letters & images
Dye inkpads in earth tones
Black inkpad by Memories
Beads
Cord

Directions: For the cover, cut the sheet of
brown paper in half widthwise. Accordion-
fold the sheet of black paper into eight
equal sections. Attach to the two cover
sheets so that the first section of the accordion fold is adhered to the front of the cover
piece and the last section of the accordion is
adhered to the front side of the back cover. .
Decorate tags and envelopes with rubber
stamps by stamping images in black. Then
use colored inkpads and a "direct-to-paper"
technique to color the envelopes, tags and
tag strings. Attach beads to tag strings.
Adhere tags and envelopes to the accordion
folds.

Jewelry

This wearable art represents a bold "next step" taken by innovative designers. Components such as watch parts, glass jewelry, and photos make unexpected and charming additions. Faux soldering mimics the look of stained glass.

WATCH FACE DOLLY
By Barbara De Lap

Black shrink plastic
Brilliance inkpads
Diamond Glaze
Watch parts & face
Hand & feet charms
1/8" hole punch
Jump rings
Assorted rubber stamps
Paper doll stamp by Limited Edition Rubber Stamps
E6000 glue
Button with flat front & shank back
Leather cording or ribbon

Directions: Stamp the paper doll stamp on the black shrink plastic using gold Brilliance ink. Let air dry, then cut the doll out. Trim off hands and feet of the doll (see photo). Using a small hole punch, punch holes at ends of arms, shoulder area of torso, bottom of torso, and tops of the legs. Using rubber stamps with a clock or watch theme, stamp all over the shrink plastic using the Brilliance inkpads. Shrink the plastic according to the manufacturer's directions. When cool, place the torso on a flat surface. Sprinkle the watch parts over the body of the torso. Place drops of Diamond Glaze over the watch parts. Be careful not to cover punched holes. Let dry for about two hours. Attach the watch face to the head of the doll using E6000 glue. Dry overnight. To assemble doll, use jump rings to attach the arms and legs to the torso and attach hand and shoe charms. Glue flat side of button to the back of the doll's head. Let dry, then place a piece of cording or ribbon through the shank to complete your necklace.

ULTRA-THICK EMBOSSING ENAMEL: The dimensional look of metal or clay can be mimicked using Ultra-Thick embossing Enamel (UTEE) or Amazing Glaze, which are large-granule embossing powders. Using a heat tool, heat the powder until it melts. Repeat the process, building layers until desired thickness has been achieved. At this point, the melted powders have a glass-like surface. An image can be impressed into the melted area with a rubber stamp while the powders are still hot. The stamp must remain in place until cooled. When creating the faux soldering look below, be sure to distribute your layers of paper evenly and use text weight paper whenever possible. This keeps the finished pieces thin and makes the dipping process easier.

FAUX SOLDERING COLLAGES
By Barbara De Lap and Sue Astroth

2 pieces thin glass (microscope slides)
Melting pot
Ultra Thick Embossing Enamel (UTEE): black, platinum, or gold enamel
Various elements for collage
Binder clip
Non-stick craft sheet
Waxed paper
Self-adhesive pin back

Directions: Do a simple collage on cardstock using a glue stick to hold pieces in place. While making the collage piece, pre-heat the pot with the UTEE of your choice. Platinum works great with this technique as it mimics true soldering. Sandwich your collage pieces between the two glass pieces. Hold together with binder clip. Hold this collage "sandwich" carefully but firmly, and dip one side into melted UTEE. Carefully lift the piece straight up then rotate your hand so that any stray UTEE drops go back into the pot. Move the clamp and repeat for all four sides. Use caution since melted UTEE is very hot. Let cool on non-stick craft sheet. If you are unhappy with the look, you can let the piece cool, and remove what you don't like and dip again. Add pin back to finish.

OPTICAL LENS NECKLACE
By Barbara De Lap

Antique optical lens
Assorted elements for collage
Cardstock: black or cream
Diamond Glaze
Small alphabet rubber stamps
Leather cording
Brilliance inkpads

Directions: Trace around lens on cardstock. Cut out on the inside of the traced circle. Do a simple collage on this cardstock using a glue stick to hold pieces in place. Let dry. Apply a nickel size amount of Diamond Glaze on one side of the glass optical lens. Place the collage piece on glass on the Diamond Glaze side, centering it with top piece. Use firm pressure and work from the middle out, pressing out any bubbles that you can see from the front. Let piece dry. Attach cording to hole at the top of the optical lens.

INTERCHANGEABLE POLYMER CLAY LOCKET
By Barbara De Lap

Pearl polymer clay
Lazertran Silk
Flip-top locket
Sculpey Glaze

Directions: Take the Lazertran to a photo copy store. Make copies of the images you wish to transfer. The copies must be made on a dry toner color copy machine, not an inkjet copies. Condition clay using a pasta machine set at the thickest setting. Trim clay to fit the inside of the locket. Transfer your image onto the clay using the Lazertran copies and following the manufacturer's directions. Bake the clay as directed. Once the tiles have cooled, use Sculpey Glaze to seal the tile. The locket is deep enough to accommodate two tiles to display a picture on both the front and back.

Ephemera

Bits of "this and that," ephemera can be anything that has meaning to you: a ticket, game piece, souvenir, old key or lucky charm. Whether art pieces or personal trinkets, found objects and memorabilia add a graphic and dynamic touch to your projects.

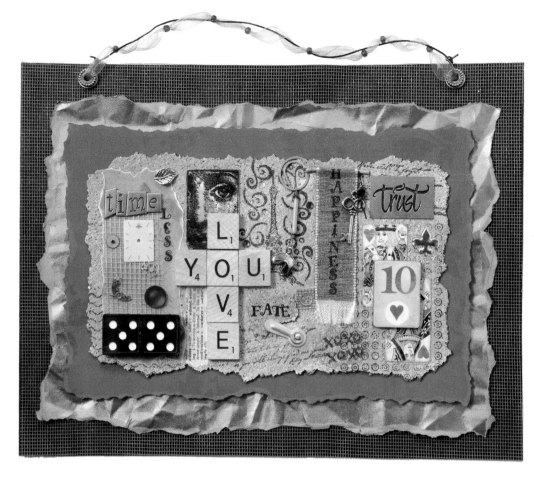

TEXTURED COLLAGE
By Traci Bautista

Black textured cardstock
Ecru cardstock
Assorted textured, patterned & handmade
    papers
Xyron machine with adhesive cartridge
Glitter & micro beads
Pearl-Ex powders
Acrylic varnish & stiff bristle brush
Chinese coin & game token
Eyelets & eyelet tools
Diamond Glaze

Directions: Run cardstock through Xyron machine to apply adhesive. Tear assorted coordinating papers into small pieces. Randomly adhere torn pieces to the ecru cardstock, leaving spaces in between papers. About half the area should be covered. In remaining area, sprinkle glitter, micro beads and metallic pigments. Press embellishments into paper with brush which has been loaded with varnish. To set, drip diamond glaze over glitter and micro beads. Let dry. Cut a 1/2" strip of the collage and attach with two eyelets. Adhere collage to black cardstock with double-sided tape. Glue Chinese coin and game token to collage with tacky glue.

HAPPY 10TH ANNIVERSARY
By Linda Lavasani

Thin cork board torn, to 6" x 9"
Black poster board & various cardstock
Gold metallic paint
Soft window screen
Various stamps
Inkpads: black, red
Alphabet charms by Making Memories
Gold Mesh
Vellum
Miscellaneous cards, game & watch parts
Rhinestones, brads, washers, & beads
Ribbon, leather cording
Beads
Heavy-duty adhesive

Directions: Paint a thin coat of gold paint on cork board. Arrange meaningful embellishments and stamped items as desired. Adhere with heavy-duty adhesive. Layer cork and papers using foam spacers to add dimension. Add to screen and poster board layers and adhere. Make hanger out of ribbon, leather cording, and beads. Attach hanger using the washers and beads.

TIC-TAC-TOE BOARD
By Sandi Marr

Pre-made wooden tic-tac-toe board
Various game pieces, cards, etc.
Gaming stamps

Directions: Use a pre-made tic-tac-toe board and paint the board black. Use photocopies of a Scrabble game, stamped game pieces, and real game pieces such as Bingo markers, dominoes, dice, playing cards, etc. to decorate the interior spaces of the board. Add ribbon for a hang tie.

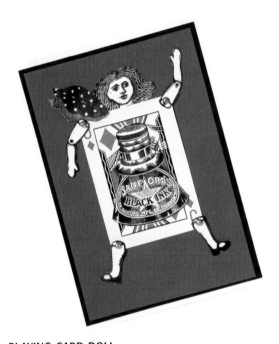

PLAYING CARD DOLL
By Krista Camacho

Cardstock: white, black, red
Rubber stamp by A Stamp in the Hand
Black inkpad
Playing card
Mini brads

Directions: Cut and fold white cardstock to 5" x 7". Cut black layer measuring $4^{1}/_{2}$" x $6^{1}/_{2}$". Cut red layer measuring $4^{1}/_{4}$" x $6^{1}/_{4}$". Stamp images on a separate sheet of white cardstock and cut out. Attach arms and legs to playing card using mini brads. Layer ink bottle image on playing card. Attach head and wings. Assemble card with adhesive.

PRIDE
By Jennifer Gaub

Cardstock: green, cream, kraft
Manila shipping tag
Patterned paper
Inkpads in brown tones
Black & white gingham ribbon
Postage stamp punch
Stipple brush
Plastic wrap
Rubber stamp alphabet letters

Directions: Start by giving the paper an aged look. Crumple the cream photo mat and tag. Iron flat, then brush dark brown inkpad over them. Drag edges of tag along inkpad to tint them. Tap bristles of stipple brush on light brown inkpad then stipple kraft paper. Punch stippled paper 5 times with postage stamp punch. With medium brown ink, stamp the word, "pride" on the punched shapes. Adhere torn piece of green patterned paper and letters to the tag as shown. Crumple sheet of plastic wrap into a ball. Dab ball onto inkpads, then onto the cream journaling page. Journal. Color the ribbon by pushing sections of it on the inkpads before gluing it to the page.

Hot Glue & Clay

Hot glue certainly isn't just for making holiday wreaths anymore; it's now a legitimate art medium in its own right. Molded materials such as lightweight paper clay and polymer clays are also finding their place in paper crafts today.

BY THE SEA
By DeAnne Velasco Musiel

Decorative papers by Creative Imaginations
Colored hot glue by Rubba Dub Dub
Hot glue gun and glue mat
Opal Fru Fru by Rubba Dub Dub
Seahorse die cut
Letter Stencil by EK Success
Pearl-Ex Powders by Jacquard

Directions: Trim two squares from map paper. Tear one side and adhere both squares to background. Trim rectangle of dark cardstock and adhere to background. Trim two strips from gradated paper. Tear one and adhere both at edges. On glue mat, dispense large puddle of teal colored glue. Let cool. Use stencil to trace letters onto glue. Trim out letters with knife. Reheat letters with heat tool and sprinkle heated glue with opal Fru Fru. Heat letters until Fru Fru melts. When cool, dust letters with Pearl-Ex. Attach letters to page. On glue mat, dispense colored glue. To make sea horses and achieve marbled effect, use two glue guns, each with a different color. Using a glue mat and alternating colors, dispense first one color, then the other in a continuous mass, until you have a size slightly smaller than your die cut. Reheat the mass with a heat gun. When fluid, cover mass with second glue mat and flatten using a book or other flat solid object. Let cool. Die cut. Attach die cuts to pages. Print journaling on vellum. Trim with decorative scissors and adhere to page. Attach photos.

HOW DOES YOUR GARDEN GROW
By DeAnne Velasco Musiel

Colored vellums
Glitter vellum by K & Co.
Floral paper by PSX
Hot glue gun
Colored hot glue by Rubba Dub Dub
Flower molds by Rubba Dub Dub
Pouring water stamp by Rubba Dub Dub
Glue mat
Clear embossing fluid
Pearl-Ex by Jacquard
Glazes by Golden
Watercolor pencils & brush
Sand inkpad by Memories

Directions: Coat sunflower mold with clear embossing fluid, then fill with hot glue. Let cool and remove from mold. Make more flowers. Dust flowers with Pearl-Ex powders. Tear floral paper. On torn edge, color with watercolor pencils then blend with wet brush. Attach to background paper. Trim glitter vellum with decorative scissors. Attach to background journaling piece and add journaling. Tint with glazes then stamp 'pouring water' stamp in sand ink over the journaling and attach to background. Print title on vellum and trim with deckle scissors before attaching. Arrange and adhere photo and molded shapes.

*H*OT *G*LUE: *Hot glue has many more uses than its ability to adhere items. Colored and metallic glues can be blended marbled, stamped and molded for many design applications. Molds and rubber stamps should be coated with clear embossing fluid so that the cooled glue will release readily. Dusting glue pieces with Pearl-Ex powder adds luster. When reheated, it can be reshaped. Write titles and make free-form designs in hot glue.*

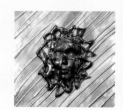

CAPTURED FEATHER
By Linda Lavasani

Black cardstock
Suede paper
Feather stamps by Stamp Zia
Black Memories inkpad
Light colored inkpad
Pearl-Ex powders & soft brush
Black polymer clay
Metallic Rub-on by Rub 'n' Buff
Spray fixative

Directions: Cut black cardstock and fold for card base. For next layer, cut black cardstock ¼" smaller than base card on all side. Press the light colored inkpad (which should be slightly dry) on this piece, one small area at a time. Quickly brush on Pearl-Ex powders and blend. Continue until the entire piece is decorated. Seal with spray fixative. Stamp small feather with black ink as shown. Trim corners. Stamp large feather on suede paper with black ink and cut out. Make circular buckle of polymer clay rolled to ⅛" thick. Texture surface with point of a paintbrush and bake to specifications. Burnish with metallic Rub-On. Layer items and adhere.

JUST MY TYPE DOLL
By Barbara De Lap

Wooden printer's type piece about 2" tall
Pearl polymer clay
Face mold
20-gauge craft wire
Beads
Hands & feet charms

Directions: Drill a hole lengthwise through the piece of wood type. Drill another hole horizontally for the arms. Run a piece of wire through the first hole, leaving enough to accommodate both legs and the polymer head, with a loop at the top for cording. Alternate threading black and white beads and add a foot charm. Run the wire back up through the beads and wrap wire around the top of the beads next to the wood type. Repeat for the other leg. and for the arms. Make a polymer clay head bead by conditioning the clay and rolling into a ball. Gently press into a face mold. Remove and bake to manufacturer's specifications. Drill hole through top of head. Run the wire through the hole, making a loop at the top for cording. Bend arms and legs into a playful position. Trim wire close with wire cutters.

EGYPTIAN PYRAMIDS
By Janis Ramsden

Cardstock: rust, black
Kraft paper
Rust mulberry paper
Paper clay
Pyramid & texture stamps
Egyptian Hieroglyphics stamp by JudiKins
Paper cording
Metallic Rub-Ons
Rust inkpad
Southwest corner punch by Marvy

Directions: Stamp unlinked texture stamp onto a flattened piece of paper clay. Stamp over the top of the texture with the pyramid stamp. When paper clay is dry, rub it with a dark color from the Rub-On set. Then rub with metallic Rub-On. Stamp hieroglyphics on beige cardstock with rust ink. Layer black cardstock on square rust card. Add rust mulberry paper with torn edges, then the stamped paper. Cut a small rectangle of rust slightly larger than pyramid piece and punch corners with southwest corner punch. Position two strips of black cardstock under sides of rust rectangle. Adhere to card as well as piece of torn mulberry paper, cording and paper clay.

FALLING AGAIN
By DeAnne Velasco Musiel

Linen texture cardstock
Square punch
Colored hot glue by Rubba Dub Dub
Pearl-Ex powder
Variegated gold leaf flakes & soft brush
Glazes by Golden
Palette paper
Hot glue gun & glue mat
Soft brushes

Directions: On palette paper, dispense 3-4 colors of glaze. Using palette knife, wipe glazes across linen textured cardstock for background. Let dry. Punch photos and cardstock with square punch. Arrange squares and adhere to page. Print or write title on plain paper. Place underneath glue mat. Trace lettering with tip of hot glue gun. When title cools a bit, brush gold leaf over parts of the title. Brush away excess with a soft brush. Place title on page and gently reheat with heat gun to adhere. Print large words on a transparency. Adhere to page. Attach main photo and dribble colored hot glue on edges. Add journaling with gel pen.

Mosaics & Tearing

Composing mosaics from paper and tearing papers for a dimensional and graphic effect are easy ways to make a fresh impression. Plus, they're a great way to use up those odds and ends of lovely paper you can't bear to part with.

SUNNY BUNNY
By Sandi Allan

Cardstock in coordinating colors
Decorative chalks

Directions: Arrange cropped photos and computer generated journaling on page. Cut strips of contrasting colored papers and cut into diagonal pieces to make a fun mosaic effect. Glue one area at a time until the entire page is filled. Add chalk to mosaic pieces to complement color scheme.

ON THE BEACH
By Sandi Allan

Cardstock
Vellum
Sepia-toned photos
Chalks
Photo coloring pens

Directions: Color sepia-toned photos of kids with photo coloring pens and cut out. Using various shades of paper and vellum make beach, wave, and sun design. Chalk the edges of the torn paper. Adhere waves first, then photos, and finally the beach for a three-dimensional effect.

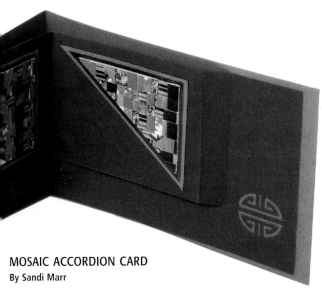

CELTIC SQUARES AND LAYERS
By Kathy Yee

Cardstock: light green, dark green
Celtic Stamp Cube #1 by JudiKins
Gold pigment inkpad
Malachite embossing powder by JudiKins
Copper & detail gold embossing powder

Directions: Adhere a background of dark green cardstock to a folded light green card. Adhere a smaller light green cardstock piece to the dark green. On another piece of light green cardstock, stamp the "square" knot with gold pigment ink eight times. Emboss with malachite embossing powder. Repeat the stamping using metallic copper embossing powder, then using detail gold embossing powder. Cut out the squares close to the embossed edge. Arrange 12 squares, four of each color on the light green cardstock, alternating colors. Make sure the squares are spaced evenly; adhere. Using decorative edged scissors, cut the remaining squares diagonally. Mount the cut squares using foam mounting tape onto the 12 glued squares. Alternate colors and corners.

ASIAN SQUARES AND LAYERS
By Kathy Yee

Cardstock: plum, metallic gold
Scraps of mulberry, patterned paper, tissue, & Washi papers
Small Asian stamps
Metallic gold inkpad

Directions: Tear scrap papers into small pieces. Arrange in collage fashion onto 3" x 5" piece of plum cardstock so that the torn papers overlap with a diagonal layout. Allow some of the plum cardstock to show. Stamp randomly on top of the glued paper using metallic gold ink. Cut the collaged plum cardstock into 1" strips then 1" squares. Adhere the gold cardstock to the folded square plum card. Lay out 9 squares evenly and glue in place. Use the squares with the most plum showing in this first layer. Cut 5 of the remaining squares diagonally with the deckle scissors. Use one small piece of foam mounting tape on each triangle shape. Align and mount to the glued squares as shown in photo.

MOSAIC ACCORDION CARD
By Sandi Marr

1 strip of red paper 4$^{1}/_{4}$" x 25$^{1}/_{2}$"
3 pieces of black cardstock 4" x 11"
Washi paper scraps
Asian symbol punch

Directions: Fold the red paper in half then fold the ends back to the middle so you have an accordion folded paper. Fold the three black pieces of paper in half. On the first black piece, cut an opening in one end leaving $^{1}/_{2}$" around three sides. This will be the frame for the back of the card. Cut the second two black pieces 4" in from the fold and 1" up from the bottom. Score at the end of the cut, and again $^{1}/_{2}$" from that score line. Fold into a "pop out." At this point you may punch a design on the sides. Using double stick tape, attach the first strip to the back of the card. Attach the second two black pieces to the front of the card. Construct small shapes using the "mosaic technique" explained in *Greeting Card Magic* by MaryJo McGraw and attach them to the four pop out panels on the black paper. Decorate the front of the card with Washi paper and a mosaic piece.

MY DREAMS FULFILLED
By Debby DeBenedetti

Cardstock
Metal foil
Ribbon
Mini glass beads

Directions: Simple tearing and folding can create a dramatic photo layout. Use ribbon laced through punched holes and punched flower decorated with mini glass beads for accents. An addition of an embossed metal foil word punctuates the heading.

HAPPY HOLIDAYS
By Jennifer Gaub

Cardstock
Patterned papers
Printed greeting

Directions: Cut squares of patterned paper into fourths at different angles for the presents. Cut triangles from the patterned paper to make the bows. Layer and adhere.

Stamping

Stamping is "where it all started" for many of our designers and where they shine artistically. The techniques on the next four pages will inspire you to explore new possibilities when using your favorite stamps and ink and bring your designs to a higher level.

KOI POND
By Linda Lavasani

Cardstock: white, red glossy, black glossy
Koi stamp by Stamp Zia
Sea grass by Posh Impressions
Square stamp & Chinese seal meaning "fish" by Red Pearl
Rock stamp
Inkpads: black, dark green, red, gold
Color Box Cat's Eye Cocoa, Burnt Copper & Topaz
Radiant Pearls in Solar Bronze, Honey Mustard, Fire Opal, Black Organza, Gold & Mink White
Black poster board
Heavy-duty double-sided tape
Spray fixative

Directions: Run a piece of removable tape 1³/₈" away from the left to right and bottom edge of an 8¹/₂" x 6¹/₂" piece of white cardstock, leaving a space at the top and bottom for the stamped squares. Refer to photo for placement of all stamped images. Lightly ink in both areas using the "direct to paper" method with Cocoa and Topaz inks. Stamp two rows of squares using Burnt Copper. Remove tape and place it along the same line, this time covering the stamped squares. Stamp two koi fish in the center area. Make a mask for the fish and cover the stamped fish. Fill in the background with gold ink using "direct to paper" technique. Leaving fish masks in place, remove tape and let dry. Stamp the sea grass image with dark green ink and highlight using Gold Radiant Pearls. Stamp three rocks along the bottom in black and add shadows around the rocks and sea grass. Paint the fish using Radiant Pearls. Stamp the Chinese seal fish image using red ink. Seal with spray fixative. Stamp an 8¹/₂" x 11" piece of white cardstock with one row of square stamps all the way around. Cut red glossy 6³/₄" x 8³/₄" and black glossy 7¹/₄" x 9¹/₄" cardstock then layer all the pieces as shown on top of black poster board.

KIMONO
By Diana Diaz

Cardstock: white, black, metallic gold
Kimono stamp by JudiKins
Cherry blossoms stamp
Acetate
Graphite Black Brilliance inkpad
Variegated gold leaf flakes
Stiff bristle brush

Directions: Stamp cherry blossoms stamp on opposite corners of white cardstock. Stamp kimono image on acetate or transparency film, using black graphite inkpad. Let dry thoroughly. Trim close to image and run through a Xyron machine using adhesive cartridge. Peel off backing. Press gold leaf onto adhesive side. Remove excess gold leaf flakes with a stiff brush. Assemble layers and adhere.

GOLD LEAF DRAGONFLY
By Diana Diaz

Cardstock: dark green, medium green, white
Dragonfly stamp by Rubbermonger
Small dragonfly stamp by Rubbernecker
Splatter stamp
Variegated gold leaf flakes
Stiff bristle brush
Gold leafing pen by Krylon
Metallic gold inkpad
Gold thread
Graphite Black Brilliance inkpad
Gold metallic inkpad

Directions: Stamp dragonfly on acetate or transparency film using black graphite pad. Let dry thoroughly. Cut out close to image. Run through a Xyron machine using adhesive cartridge. Peel off backing. Press gold leaf onto adhesive side. Remove excess gold leaf flakes with a stiff brush. Stamp background dragonflies with gold inkpad on white cardstock. Stamp splatter background on card using gold Encore inkpad. Assemble layers and adhere. Attach dragonfly. Punch two small holes on crease of card and add cording.

LION
By Diana Diaz

Cardstock
Grass cloth paper
Glossy white cardstock
Black inkpad by Memories
Lion stamp
Pens #451, #985, & #991 by Tombow

Directions: Stamp lion on glossy paper using black inkpad. Let dry completely, then color background using Tombow pen #451. Color lion using pen #991; make long strokes, being careful not to add too much color. Use pen #985 to highlight. Layer cardstock and grass cloth and adhere.

PEAR
By Sue Astroth

Cardstock: dark green, cream, kraft
Inkpads: ochre, black, green
Blender pen by Dove
Gold leafing pen by Krylon
Watercolor pencils
Script stamp by Stamp in the Hand
Pear stamp by Rubber Stampede
Stipple brushes

Directions: Cut one piece kraft cardstock 3" x 11". Fold in half, using a bone folder. Stamp pear on cream cardstock in black ink. With colored pencils, color the outlines and shaded area of pear. Go over entire pear with blender pen to create a watercolor effect. Stipple pear with ochre ink. Cut out. Stamp script in black on cream cardstock and trim. Stipple with green ink. Lightly edge with gold leafing pen. Cut two pieces of green cardstock. Edge each with gold leafing pen. Layer as shown in picture, use foam dot spacers to attach pear giving added dimension.

VICTORIAN GIRL
By Diana Diaz

Cardstock: white, lavender, purple, gold
Flower print paper
Black inkpad by Brilliance
Victorian girl stamp by Magenta
Radiant Pearls
Decorative chalk

Directions: Stamp Victorian girl with black ink on white cardstock. Color in with cotton swab and decorative chalks. Add luster to cummerbund with Radiant Pearls. Layer cardstock and papers as shown and adhere.

CLASSIC CARS
By Phyllis Nelson

Cardstock: black, white
Postage stamps with car images
Rubber stamps of vintage cars
Rubber stamps of postage cancellations
Colored cardstock for layering
Black inkpad
Watercolor markers or colored pencils
Fiskars postage scissors

Directions: Stamp the classic car images on white cardstock with black ink. Shade the images softly with color using watercolor markers or colored pencils. Cut out the cars with the postage scissors. Layer the car images on colored cardstock. Cut a thin strip of black paper and glue it down the side of the white card. Alternating real postage stamps and the stamped pieces, glue them down the length of the card. Add stamped cancellation marks over some of the designs.

BUTTERFLIES
By Terrece Siddoway

Cardstock: white, blue, camel
Butterfly stamp
Black watercolor inkpad
Watercolor pencils
Markers

Directions: Stamp image on white cardstock using black inkpad. Color butterflies with watercolor pencils with a medium hand, starting where you want the color darkest. Blend with a wet paint brush or water brush. Let dry. Enhance outlines and black areas with markers. Mount on blue and camel cardstock as shown.

LOVE BIRDS
By Linda Lavasani

Cardstock: white, dark green, gold metallic
Dove stamp by Beeswax
Small branch stamp
Aspen Leaf Stamp by JudiKins
Radiant Pearls
Fresh Greens inkpad
   by Kaleidacolor
Black inkpad by StazOn
Decorative corner punch
Gold foil & foil adhesive
Ribbons & threads
Beads
Spray fixative

Directions: Cut dark green cardstock to make a square when folded. Stamp the doves on white cardstock in black ink. Paint the stamped area with Radiant Pearls. Seal each layer with spray fixative. Outline outer edge with gold foil using adhesive. Cut out image leaving a thin border. Make layers of cardstock colors, punch corners and stamp backgrounds. Use Radiant Pearls to fill in color. Assemble layers and finish with ribbon threads and beads.

> *STAMPING: Ink your stamp with the appropriate ink for the job. Dye-based inks are water-based, sheer and quick drying. Pigment-based inks are opaque and are raised if used with embossing powders. These powders may be clear, pearlized, metallic, or iridescent. Permanent ink is solvent based and can be used on non-porous surfaces like photos.*

ELEGANT GEISHA
By Kathy Yee

Cardstock: black, gold, cream, soft metallic
Washi paper, gold decorative paper
Chinese lady stamp by Stamp Francisco
Black inkpad by Memories
Radiant Pearls: Wacky Walnut, Oyster Shell, Mayan Gold & colors to match Washi paper
Greek border punch by Fiskars
Gold foil & adhesive
Foam mounting tape

Directions: Stamp the lady with black ink onto the cream cardstock. Let ink dry before coloring. Mount the gold cardstock to the black card. Mount the Washi paper over the left side of the gold cardstock. Punch the right side edge of the gold cardstock with the border punch. Adhere the stamped image to another piece of black cardstock then mount to the card using foam-mounting tape. Paint the lady with Radiant Pearls. Begin with the flesh color for the face and hands using one part Wacky Walnut and two parts Oyster Shell. Use other colors of Radiant Pearls to match the Washi paper. Point the tip of the brush to the outside edge of the kimono. Paint around the image. Wet the paintbrush and blot off the excess moisture. Draw the Radiant Pearls from the edges to the middle of the image with the dry brush. Dilute the Mayan Gold paint and highlight some of the lines and folds of the image. Blot excess Radiant Pearls paint. Put the gold foil adhesive on the hair decoration, earrings, and belt. Let dry until tacky. Apply the gold foil, shiny side up, on the adhesive and rub gently. Pull away and burnish.

RADIANT PEARLS: Radiant Pearls are semi-translucent paints which are easy to blend and layer. They can be applied with a paintbrush, stipple brush or fingers. Since they are water-soluble, water is sufficient for clean-up. Brushes must be thoroughly dry before switching colors. Absorbent paper is a good choice for use with Radiant Pearls. Coated or glossy papers and vellum may be used, but drying times will vary. Radiant Pearls will not dry on plastic— ever! Therefore, acrylic sheets, transparencies, or compact disks make great palettes.

EYE ON KNOWLEDGE
By Terrece Siddoway

Cardstock in coordinating colors
Variegated cardstock
Pigment inkpads by Colorbox
Assorted stamps
Black inkpad by Memories
Pear stamp by Stamper's Anonymous

Directions: Using "direct to paper" technique (see page 40), apply pigment colors to mottled cardstock. Stamp various word stamps over the paper. Stamp face last. Repeat on a second piece of cardstock then stamp main pear image. Cut out and attach to upper left hand corner. Assemble graduated sizes of complementary cardstock squares. Adhere with double-sided tape.

OLD WEST
By Terrece Siddoway

Rust cardstock
Patterned paper
Old West image
Black inkpad
Colored pencils by Prismacolor

Directions: Stamp image on rust colored paper using a black inkpad. Color image with colored pencils. Use light colors to make bright areas pop. Opaque pencil coverage brightens the image. Add saying at bottom if desired. Layer and adhere as shown.

Heat Embossing

Let's heat it up and go a step further! To take your stamping designs to the next level, try materials such as embossing powders, gold leafing, acetate, and enhancements such as decorative chalks, radiant pearls and clear lacquer.

BLACK AND GOLD
By Phyllis Nelson

Cardstock: red, black
Medallion stamp by JudiKins
Gold embossing powder & embossing pad
Gold threads
Silver gel pen

Directions: Stamp and emboss the medallion stamp with gold powder. Color as shown with a silver gel pen. Cut out the image. Tear the edge of one side of the square black card. Brush the torn edges with an embossing pad and emboss with gold powder. Cut red cardstock into a square slightly smaller than the black card. Cut five small slits on the top and bottom of the red card for the gold thread. Tape the gold thread onto the back of the card, then wind it around the card, catching it in the slits. Cut the thread and tape down on the back of the card. Tear one side of the red paper and attach to the black card. Glue medallion on top of the threads.

EMBOSSING: This technique gives stamping raised and textured effects for dramatic surface interest. Clear, colored, or metallic embossing powders are dusted on wet inked areas. The excess is shaken off. A heat gun or embossing heat tool is used to melt the powder. Powders are available in a tempting array of colors and textures.

COLLAGE GEISHA KIMONO
By Kathy Yee

Cardstock: gold, black, white
Mulberry & Washi papers
Black & gold marbled paper
Geisha stamp
Black inkpad
Clear embossing powder
Watercolor markers
Kimono template
Wooden skewer
Paper crimper
Foam mounting tape

Directions: Stamp geisha with black ink on white cardstock. Emboss with clear powder. Color the geisha with markers. Cut out a kimono shape from black cardstock. Tear mulberry and Washi papers into small pieces and adhere randomly on the kimono. Tear stamped geisha and glue to the collaged kimono. Using tape, attach two strips of marbled paper on each side of the kimono to resemble pleats. Attach wooden skewer to the back of the kimono. Crimp gold cardstock and adhere to black paper, then to the gold card. Attach the kimono with foam mounting tape.

ASIAN COIN
By Kathy Yee

Cardstock: black, cream, rust
Gold decorative paper
Assorted Asian stamps
Black & gold pigment inkpads
Adirondack Terra Cotta inkpad
Detail gold & detail clear embossing powder
1/8" hole punch
Gold embroidery floss
Mini-envelope template

Directions: Stamp background images with Terra Cotta ink on cream cardstock. Adhere to black folded card. Stamp butterfly, leaf, Asian seal, and two Asian coins with black pigment ink on rust cardstock. Emboss with clear powder and cut out images leaving a small border. Punch a 1/8" hole in the top of each coin. Trace mini-envelope template on rust cardstock. Cut out and score on fold lines with bone folder. Stamp images randomly on outside of envelope with black ink. Use envelope template, trace the top envelope flap and the interior of the envelope on the back of the gold decorative paper. Cut out and glue to the inside of the envelope, leaving a small border of the envelope around the flap. Fold sides of envelope and adhere. Wrap gold floss around the envelope. Adhere envelope, butterfly, leaf, and seal to card. Attach punched coin to each end of the gold floss. From black cardstock, cut a small rectangle. Stamp Chinese character with gold pigment ink. Emboss with detail gold embossing powder. Tuck card into envelope and attach.

BAMBOO KIMONO
By Kathy Yee

Cardstock: black, gold
Self-adhesive acetate
Bamboo kimono stamp by JudiKins
Background #2 by Art Impressions
Happiness symbol stamp
Black inkpad by Memories
Gold metallic inkpad
Detail gold embossing powder
Gold cord
Small tassel
Perfect Pearls Pastel Set by Ranger

Directions: Fold the front top right corner of the black card diagonally to the folded side. Score a line 1" from the first fold toward the top right corner and fold back toward the top right corner. Stamp the background with metallic gold inkpad randomly on the bottom front of the card. Adhere a gold strip to the first fold and a gold triangle to the second fold. Stamp the "happiness" character on the top right side of the card with the metallic gold pad and emboss with gold powder. Stamp the kimono on acetate, using the black dye-based ink and heat set with heat gun. Cut out kimono leaving 1/8" border all around. Remove backing from acetate and, using a brush, apply small amounts of 3–4 different colors of Perfect Pearls on the acetate. Tie the tassel and gold cord around the kimono. Adhere the kimono to the front of the card with double-sided tape.

CHRISTMAS HOLLY
By Janis Ramsden

Cardstock: kraft, gold metallic, green
Holly stamp by Magenta
Gold embossing powder & embossing ink
Southwest corner punch
Green & red watercolor markers
Clear crystal lacquer

Directions: Punch corners of gold paper. Stamp holly onto kraft paper with gold and emboss. Cut out along edge. Color in green and red areas. Use dot of clear crystal lacquer on each red berry. Adhere to gold paper then layer on green cardstock with adhesive.

BEES
By Diana Diaz

Cardstock: white, yellow, black
Patterned paper
Bee stamp & frame stamp
Black inkpads
Clear embossing powder
Watercolor markers
Decorative scissors
Glitter

Directions: Stamp bee and frame on white paper using black pigment inkpad. Emboss with clear powder. Cut around frame with decorative scissors. Color frame and bee with yellow pen. Layer frame on polka dot and yellow papers. Cut 1¹/₄" from front of black card. Cut bee paper to fit as shown and adhere to black card. Cut thin yellow strip of paper and adhere to edge of trimmed card. Cut out three bees from paper and glue to right side of inside exposed card. Apply glitter to bee.

ASIAN VASE
By Diana Diaz

Cardstock
Decorative paper
Flower punches, small dot, & swirl punch
Gold tinsel embossing powder
Vase stamp by Great Impressions

Directions: Stamp vase on cardstock using clear embossing pad and gold tinsel embossing powder. Cut out and layer papers as shown. Cut out leaves in various sizes. Punch out flowers and add small punched dots. Using a toothpick to apply glue, adhere pieces to background.

GOLDEN LEAF
By Sue Astroth

Cardstock: olive green, metallic green,
   black
Leaf stamp by Stamp in Hand
Gold pigment ink
Gold embossing powder
Decorative edge scissors

Directions: Stamp and emboss leaf on a piece of black cardstock. Cut a piece of metallic green cardstock with decorative edge scissors. Cut a piece of olive green cardstock and fold in half. Layer as shown in photo.

REINDEER ORNAMENT
By Sue Astroth

Cardstock: black, cream
Rectangle papier maché ornament
Alphabet stamps by Hero Arts
Reindeer stamp by Uptown Designs
Script stamp for background
Deckle edge scissors
Red-violet & copper Lumiere paint
Gold embossing powder & embossing pad
Black inkpad
¹/₄" black satin ribbon, 18" length

Directions: Paint papier maché ornament with copper and paint a half sheet of cream cardstock with red-violet; let dry. Stamp reindeer twice on cream and emboss with gold. Cut out. Layer on black and cut out again. Stamp "joy" twice in black on small scrap of cream cardstock; cut out. Layer on black. Stamp script on remainder of cream cardstock. Deckle cut two pieces script background. Cut out two pieces of painted cardstock. Tear two pieces of black cardstock to mat the script background. Following photo, layer pieces on both sides of ornament. Tie black satin ribbon around ornament hanger.

JAPANESE FAN
By Susan Gin

Cardstock: purple, black, white, gold
Fan stamp by Limited Edition
Crane background stamp by JudiKins
Embossing pad
Pearl & gold embossing powder
Heavy-weight vellum
Gold hot glue stick and glue gun
Seal for hot glue by JudiKins
Pearl-Ex interference powders in blue &
**   violet**
Gum arabic
Slide tassel
Black pigment inkpad

Directions: Stamp and emboss the crane background using pearl embossing powder on heavy-weight vellum. Trim the edges and layer onto white cardstock and then on purple paper. Attach to a black card. Emboss the fan image using gold embossing powder on a piece of black cardstock. Paint the fan using Pearl-Ex blue and violet interference powders which have been mixed with water and a small amount of gum arabic. Cut the embossed piece into a square. Layer the fan rectangle on gold cardstock, then on black. Prepare the seal by stamping it on a black pigment inkpad. Melt a piece of hot glue over the top loop of the tassel onto the top of the card. Immediately press the seal down to make the crane impression. Attach the fan piece over the top of the tassel with double-stick tape. Use double-sided tape on the back of the fan to adjust the length of the tassel and attach.

> *PEARL-EX can be dusted over still-wet stamped images provided it is then sprayed with a fixative. It can be mixed with water and gum arabic for use as a transparent watercolor paint. Add it to any viscous medium to give artwork a colorfast pearlescent or metallic luster. Gold leafing also adds an undeniable richness. Use gold leaf adhesive glue or double-sided tapes to adhere leafing to accent areas of your creations.*

JAPANESE LONG LIFE
By Phyllis Nelson

Cardstock: black, purple
Japanese handmade papers
Gold Momi paper
Embossing pad & gold powder
Metallic gel pens in purple & silver
Floral stamp by Magenta
Long Life character stamp by Stamp Oasis
Gold ink pen
Purple metallic cord

Directions: Stamp the floral image on a piece of black cardstock and emboss using gold powder. Color the flowers with a purple metallic gel pen. Color the centers and other dots in silver. Cut around the edge of the floral image, leaving 1/8" border. Wrap a band of gold Momi paper around a rectangle of white and gold Japanese paper and glue it down on the reverse. Glue the black embossed piece to the top of the white and gold papers. Cut a 10" x 7" piece of purple card stock and fold it to make the base card. Cut a piece of black paper slightly smaller than the front of the card and glue it to the center of the card. Attach a rectangle of purple printed paper to the black layer. Glue the white piece over the center of the purple print as shown. Emboss the long life character using gold powder. Position the character in the bottom right hand corner so that it overlaps the white paper. Use a gold ink pen to fill in any spaces in the embossed image. Tie a purple metallic cord to the side of the card.

Beading

Love of all things beaded has taken crafts by storm and paper craft is no exception. Beads in all their glory are sprinkled throughout this book like fairy dust. Here we highlight beads, diamond glaze, and micro-beads as glamorous accents all by themselves.

HAPPY BIRTHDAY FLOWER POT
By Phyllis Nelson

Cardstock: cream, terra cotta
White parchment
Stamps by Imaginations & Printworks
Black watercolor inkpad
Watercolor pencils & brush
Diamond Glaze by JudiKins
Sinamay mesh
E beads or seed beads

Directions: Stamp the flowerpot image on a piece of white parchment cardstock using a black watercolor inkpad. Stamp the words on a separate piece of cardstock. With the watercolor pencils, add colors to the image. With a small amount of water on the paintbrush, blend the colors and wash around the edges to create a watercolor look. After the piece has dried, tear around the edges. Tear around the words. On a cream card, layer the terra-cotta colored paper, the sinamay mesh and the stamped piece using double sided tape. Apply a small amount of Diamond Glaze to the centers of the flowers. On the glaze, arrange a group of the beads. Allow to dry.

BEADED BOX (1)
By Janis Ramsden

Papier maché box
Wooden ball feet & knob
Wonder tape
Beedz by Art Accents
Acrylic metallic paint
Gold leaf flakes & adhesive
Fibers
Lacquer sealer

Directions: Paint wood feet black. Add gold leaf adhesive randomly and apply gold leaf. Paint box inside and out with acrylic metallic paint. Attach one side of adhesive bead tape to lid sides. Peel off backing and apply beads. Attach painted bead to top and add fibers. Glue feet to bottom of box and seal with lacquer.

BEADED BOX (2)
By Terrece Siddoway

Papier maché box
Wooden ball feet
Beads in two coordinating color-mixes in medium & micro sizes
Wonder tape
Acrylic metallic paint

Directions: Paint wooden balls and box inside and out with acrylic metallic paint. Once dry, apply tape to sides of box with the lid on so that you do not put the tape too high on the box. Remove lid and cover lid with tape on top and sides. Hold box from the inside and remove tape to reveal adhesive. Roll box in micro beads. Press beads into tape. Repeat process with lid using larger coordinating beads. Roll a second time in micro beads and press on. Glue ball feet to bottom of box.

BEADED PEN
By April Nelson

Pen
Wonder tape
Colored beads in medium & micro sizes
Ribbon

Directions: Apply one side of adhesive tape to pen, peel off backing and roll twice in beads. Roll first in medium-sized beads and then in micro beads. Press beads on with fingers to adhere. Add ribbon.

SNOW SCENE (DETAIL)
By Debby DeBenedetti

Cardstock
Beaded trim
Snowflake charms

Torn paper and purchased beaded trim secured on the reverse makes an attractive winter look. Sew on snowflake charms for interest.

EASTER (DETAIL)
By Debby DeBenedetti

Cardstock
Colored vellum
Eyelets & eyelet tools
Double-sided adhesive sheets
Clear micro beads
Buttons

Directions: Tear colored vellum into strips. Adhere strips to top of page and weave horizontal strips in and out of vertical strips for a woven effect. Secure all vellum ends and add eyelets on top. Cut out flowers from double-sided adhesive sheets. Peel off front side of tape and dip in clear micro-beads. Peel off backing and attach to colored cardstock. Add tiny buttons and vellum leaves.

BEADED GRAPES
By Phyllis Nelson

Cardstock
Gold paper
Grape stamp
Lattice stamp by JudiKins
Embossing pad & gold powder
Diamond Glaze by JudiKins
Clear micro beads
Watercolor markers

Directions: Stamp and emboss the grape image with gold embossing powder on light purple cardstock. Stamp the lattice background on a darker purple card and emboss with gold. Color the grapes and leaves with watercolor markers. Layer this image on gold paper. Trim to leave a small border. Glue onto olive green paper and trim with a larger border. Glue the grape piece on the card. Apply Diamond Glaze to alternate grapes. Sprinkle clear beads over the glaze and shake off excess. When dry, fill in the remainder of the grapes with glaze and repeat the beading process. This method prevents the glaze from running and gives a more defined shape to the grapes.

CANVAS PAINTING
By Sandi Marr

Canvas of desired size
Assorted word stamps
Acrylic metallic paints in variety of colors
Micro beads
Mica flakes
Clear granular gel medium
Skeleton leaves
Charms
Flat marbles
Stipple brush & sponges

Directions: Use a purchased canvas and apply a basecoat of a desired color of acrylic metallic paint. Apply clear granular gel medium to build dimension. Let dry. Using several complementary colors, apply more color with a stipple brush and sponges. Let dry. Stamp words on background in black. Apply more paint and while paint is still wet, apply micro beads and mica flakes to canvas. Add skeleton leaves, charms, marbles, etc. for added decoration.

MR. PERSONALITY
By Jennifer Gaub

Cardstock
Beads
Invisible thread

Directions: Use cardstock, photos and journaling to make page layout. Tear coordinating cardstock and wrap with invisible thread and beads for a design element. Layer and adhere to page.

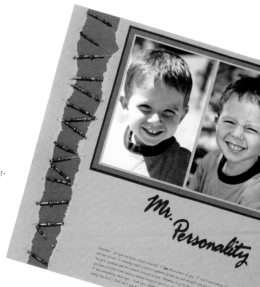

Metal & Tags

Metal accents and tags add interesting texture and new dimension to any project. Tags, a staple of the scrapbooking scene, now take their place in bookmaking and memory pages. Metal's shimmer adds dimension and a touch of pizazz.

DIRECT-TO-PAPER: One method of surface embellishment is the "direct-to-paper" technique. Gently rub the top of one or more pigment inkpads across a sheet of paper. By varying color selections and the pressure, motion and direction of one's hand during application, the resulting interplay between color combinations and textural effects is unlimited.

BLESSINGS
By Sue Astroth

Cardstock: copper, purple, ivory
Blessings stamp
Gold embossing powder
Script stamp by Stamp in the Hand
2 metal leaf cutouts
24-gauge copper wire
Foam dots

Directions: Stamp script stamp over ivory cardstock creating a background. Stamp "blessings" on ivory cardstock and emboss with gold embossing powder. Cut out. Wrap each leaf with a 9" piece of copper wire. Coil wire around pencil for added dimension. Wrap wire ends to back of leaves. Layer cardstock pieces as shown. Adhere leaves with foam dots for dimension.

APOLLO
By Jennifer Gaub

Cardstock
Patterned paper by Leisure Arts
Mulberry paper
Metal eyelet letters by Making Memories
Charms by Leisure Arts
Fibers

Directions: Arrange and layer cardstock, patterned and mulberry papers with photos across two pages and adhere. Add eyelet letters and charms on corners. Make tag shapes with photos and fibers and attach.

DREAMER
By Sandi Allan

Blue papers
Round tags
Large round punch
Vellum
Dream catcher
Feathers
Chalks

Directions: Print the word "Dreamer" in a large font to fit on tags, leaving a space between each letter to allow for punching out. Glue letters to tags and shade with chalk to match layout. Print journaling on sky vellum and layer with star printed paper and other flat items, then adhere. Attach dream catcher element with heavy-duty adhesive. (To make your own dream catcher use a 3" ring and a variety of wire, beads, leather, and feathers). Attach dream catcher, feathers and tags.

BUTTERFLY
By Janis Ramsden

Cardstock: purple, cream
Vine stamp by Great Impressions
Metal butterfly shape
Gold leaf flakes, adhesive & brush
Pearl-Ex powder
Corner rounder
Pigment inkpads: green, violet, pink, purple

Directions: Paint gold leaf adhesive on butterfly and apply gold leaf flakes. Brush off excess. Fill in with Pearl-Ex powder. Cut rectangle of cream cardstock. Using direct-to-paper technique, layer colors of ink on cardstock. Stamp vine with the purple ink for an over-all design. Cut a small square of purple. Attach strips of double-sided tape to make a square frame. Remove tape liner to expose adhesive. Press gold leaf flakes on adhesive and remove excess with soft brush. Adhere butterfly to square with adhesive dot. Cut frame from stamped piece. Layer it on the purple cardstock. Round corners of the remaining rectangle and adhere all elements as shown.

SEASONS GREETINGS
By Jennifer Gaub

Cardstock: blue, white
Snowflake paper
Round metal-rimmed tag
Square punch
Eyelet & eyelet tools
Fiber
Snowflake punch
Metallic Rub-On
Season's Greetings stamp
Blue inkpad

Directions: Adhere snowflake patterned paper to base white card. Punch large square hole in front of card. Add snowflake paper to inside of metal circle tag and punch hole at top. Add white eyelet to card and tie fiber to hold the tag to the card. Add snowflakes punched from white cardstock and add metallic Rub-Ons to blue snowflake. Add blue cardstock to the inside of the card. Decorate blue snowflake with metallic Rub-On. cut square of blue cardstock and glue to inside of card. Stamp "Season's Greetings" on white cardstock rectangle with blue inkpad. Mount on larger blue rectangle and glue to card.

DREAM, INSPIRE, IMAGINE
By Sandi Allan

Patterned papers
Word embellishments
Round tags
Metal embellishments
Eyelets & eyelet tools
Ribbon

Directions: Layer large favorite photo and papers in coordinating colors. Attach to layout page. Adhere metal embellishments to tags and small squares with eyelets. Thread sheer ribbon through round tags.

BELIEVE IN YOURSELF
By Jennifer Gaub

Cardstock
Patterned paper
Vellum tags
Apple eyelets & eyelet tools
Fibers
Rub-On title by Making Memories

Directions: Cut squares of colored cardstock. Attach vellum tags to squares with apple eyelets. Rub title onto white cardstock and tear into a rectangle. Add natural fiber and thread through tag holes. Layer all elements and adhere.

DOIN' DA EGGS (DETAIL)
By Debby DeBenedetti

Cardstock: blue, green
Patterned paper
Stamped tags
Egg punch
1/8" green satin ribbon

Torn or cut papers are layered. Egg punches dance along the edge of the patterned paper and stamped tags tied with ribbon create a fresh Easter border.

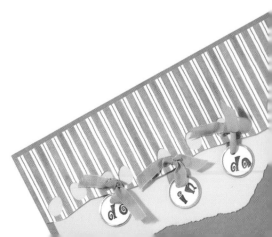

ABOUT A BOY
By Jennifer Gaub

Cardstock in assorted colors
Blue & red patterned papers
Background & texture stamps
Brown inkpad
Eyelet & eyelet tools
Jute cording

Directions: Cut tag shapes from cardstock and attach eyelets. Stamp background and texture stamps on tags using brown inkpad. Tear and glue paper pieces and computer generated focus words on tags. Add titles with a template, stamps, or computer generated font. Add gold star brads in corners to hold jute cording.

GOING TO THE ZOO
By Jennifer Gaub

Cardstock in assorted colors
Handmade paper
Letter stamps by Rubber Stampede
Animal stamps by Stampabilities
Watercolor pencils
Black inkpad & marker
Hole punch
Cording

Directions: Cut tag shapes using black ink, stamp "ZOO" letters on tags and animal stamps on cardstock. Color with watercolor pencils. Blend color with wet brush. When dry, cut rectangle shapes around animals and border with handmade paper. Punch holes in tags and outline with black pen. Layer papers, photos and journaling. Attach with adhesive. Lace cording through tags and round photo mat that has been punched with small holes.

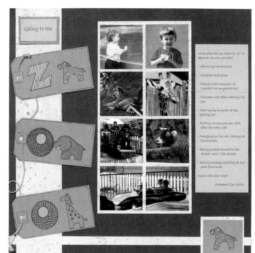

THOSE BABY BLUES
By Sandi Allan

Embossed & reversible papers
Raffia
Tags
Animal templates
Daisy punches
Chalks
Gel pens

Directions: Use assorted complimentary papers to match photos. To create layout, use templates to cut out animals and daisies from patterned paper. Outline with gel pen. Add journaling, vellum and raffia to attach tags. Hide glue spots with daisy punches in corners. Print title in a large font, cut out and glue to tags. Use chalks to shade letters and attach to background.

HAPPY BIRTHDAY
By Jennifer Gaub

Patterned paper
Dragonfly template
Square metal-rimmed tag
"Happy Birthday" stamp
Black inkpad
Multi-colored yarn

Directions: Arrange blocks of patterned papers on white base card. Cut dragonfly from template. Stamp greeting on square tag and tie on yarn. Assemble and adhere.

HAPPY BIRTHDAY TO YOU
By Jennifer Gaub

Cardstock in assorted colors
Water-based colored markers to match cardstock
Twistel by Making Memories
"Happy Birthday" stamp
Black inkpad
Tags
Hole punch

Directions: Base card is white with dots of color made with markers. Cut four tags and add squares to each top. Punch tag hole and tie off using Twistel. Stamp tags with birthday greeting. Add detail lines around tags and attach to card.

I WANT TO BE
By Sandi Allan

Cardstock
Vellum
Ribbon
Metal stars
Sewing machine
Silver thread

Directions: Cut 4" from one side of 12" x 12" cardstock. On this piece mark off five equal sections. Place on the back of the printed paper and sew sections, using a straight stitch, to make five pockets. Glue matted titles onto each section. Make tags with corresponding journaling. Punch holes in right hand edges of tags and add ribbon. Place each tag into its pocket. Glue title onto a darker matting paper. Glue on page. Glue poem with matting diagonally as shown. Embellish with stars and silver thread.

Metal Foil

Metal foil can be melded into many interesting effects from simple to ornate. Just a few humble tools are needed to make a myriad of effects: a stylus or an embossing tool and scissors are all you need to create rich-looking reticulated accents.

BIG DADDY
By Debby DeBenedetti

Cardstock: black, ecru
Letter or alphabet templates
Metal foil in copper tone
Embossing stylus
Nails by Chatterbox
Buttons
Old magazine

Directions: Cut metal foil with an allowance for trimming and folding edges under. Trim corners diagonally and fold over edges on all sides to the back. Place foil face down on an old magazine or foam core and place word templates face down on foil and trace with stylus. Adhere foil to cardstock with double-sided tape. Create journaling on computer and print on ecru cardstock. Cut around border and adhere to foil with double-sided tape. Trace and cut out date using number templates on coordinating cardstock and glue in place as shown. Attach three "nails" on each side of foil and add buttons.

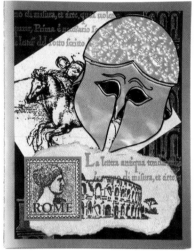

SUNFLOWER
By Diana Diaz

Brown cardstock
Sunflower stamp by Magenta
Splatter stamp
Metal foil in copper tone
Permanent black inkpad
Square panel card
Embossing stylus
Old magazine

Directions: Stamp sunflower on metal foil with black ink. Heat to speed drying. With an old magazine for padding, use a stylus to emboss the image. Turn over and dry emboss more lines as desired for texture. Cut out image, leaving a small border around the edge. Use a bone folder to smooth edges. Cut a piece of brown cardstock to fit just inside the panel card. Stamp splatters in black ink. Using a square template and stylus, emboss a frame around the brown square. Adhere card, brown panel and sunflower using double-sided tape.

POINSETTIA
By Diana Diaz

Cardstock: ecru, red, black
Stamps: Poinsettia & Merry Christmas
Black inkpad
Metal foil in red tone
Embossing stylus

Directions: Make metal poinsettia following the techniques for sunflower card (above). Stamp poinsettia in black ink on ecru paper; blot once. Stamp Merry Christmas in black ink. Layer papers on card as shown. Adhere poinsettia with double-sided tape.

MASK
By Janis Ramsden

Cardstock: black, white, ecru, metallic copper
Natural colored handmade paper
Stamps: Mask by JudiKins; Rome postoid by Toy Box; horse by Stampington & Co.; Coliseum, scripts & geometric texture stamps
Metal foil in copper tone
Copper metallic pen by Krylon
Permanent black inkpad
Metallic Rub-Ons
Embossing stylus
Inkpads: white, copper, black

Directions: Using the permanent inkpad, stamp mask on copper foil. Let dry and cut out. With an old magazine for padding, use an embossing stylus to trace around the mask lines and texture the helmet. Stamp horse figure and postoid in black on the cream paper and the coliseum on the handmade paper. Cut paper with the horse into a large square. Trim the postoid close to the image and tear around the coliseum. Highlight the postoid with the copper pen and layer onto copper paper. Apply Rub-Ons to the torn paper. Use copper paper to make the base card, layering with black. Stamp texture stamp on black paper using a white inkpad. Layer stamped paper on the card, stamping script images in copper over the layers. Adhere copper mask using double-sided tape.

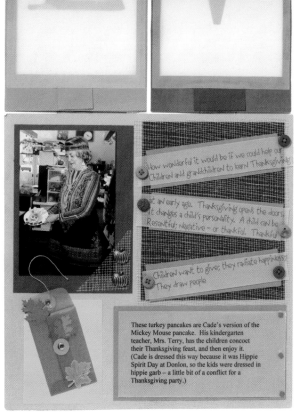

These turkey pancakes are Cade's version of the Mickey Mouse pancake. His kindergarten teacher, Mrs. Terry, has the children concoct their Thanksgiving feast, and then enjoy it. (Cade is dressed this way because it was Hippie Spirit Day at Donlon, so the kids were dressed in hippie garb – a little bit of a conflict for a Thanksgiving party.)

Thanksgiving Party 2000

OPENED

CLOSED

METAL FOIL: 38-gauge metal foil is pliable, light enough to be cut with scissors, yet it is heavy enough to keep its shape when embossed with a stylus. The foil is made from aluminum and is available in rolls and sheets. One side of the foil is artificially colored; the opposite side is the natural silver tone. Copper-tone metal foil should not be confused with copper metal which is available in a number of gauges and has its own applications.

FALL
By Debby DeBenedetti

Various cardstock & papers
Metal foil in gold tone
Vellum
Brads
Buttons
Letter tiles
Embossing stylus
Hole punch
Buttons
Charms
Miscellaneous memorabilia
Glue dots

Directions: Arrange fall photos on a background page. Computer generate over-sized letters on vellum and position each in a cardstock frame. Each letter, in its cardstock frame, will measure 6" x 12". The tags, when hinged, will flip up to reveal the photos. Make four hinges by tracing a small hinge onto the metal foil with a stylus. Cut out hinges with scissors. Punch two holes in each hinge to accommodate the brads as shown. Insert a brad in each hole. Cover the sharp ends of the brads with a cardstock square to avoid scratching the photos. Attach the vellum and cardstock frames to the page by securing the hinges with glue dots.

Wire

Wire, by itself or in combination with metal or beads, adds flare and dimension to projects. See how easily wire can be manipulated into intriguing shapes and curlicues to highlight your favorite images.

DOUBLE HEARTS
By Jennifer Gaub

Cardstock
Red mesh
Metal foil in silver tone
Stylus
Wire
Beads

Directions: Place a piece of foil (silver side down) on a mouse pad or foam core. Draw the double hearts using a small stylus. Fold over the four corners to hide raw edges. Adhere the metal to the red mesh with tape. Tear the four sides of the white cardstock mat, add small holes for wire, and mount the red mesh on top. Thread the wire through holes in the card and add beads. Curl the four ends of wire.

LOVE
By Jennifer Gaub

Cardstock: white & dark, medium, light pink
Heart punch
Page Pebbles by Making Memories
24-gauge wire
Jump rings
Cotton ball
Pink chalk

Directions: Cut a square of light pink cardstock. rub pink chalk on edges with cotton ball. Write greeting on card and add a small Page Pebble over each letter. Twist 24-gauge wire as shown making small swoops on both ends. Punch hearts and add jump rings. Attach jump rings to the wire. Make small wire "staples" to hold the wire to the card. Layer on square of dark pink cardstock and then on white card.

DRAGONFLY
By Phyllis Nelson

Black cardstock
Lavender textured paper
Dragonfly stamp from Paula Best
Embossing pad & silver embossing powder
Iridescent blue beads
Moonlight gel pens by Sakura
22-gauge silver wire
Black marker
Wooden skewer

Directions: Stamp and emboss the dragonfly in silver on black cardstock. Color in the image using gel pens. Trim around the image leaving a section at the top to accommodate the beading. Using a black marker, color the wooden skewer. Thread about nine beads on a piece of silver wire. Bend the wire at a right angle at the end of the section of beads. Push the wire ends from the front of the cardstock through to the back. Draw wire ends up, then wind it around the skewer from the two sides. Cut the wire. Layer the beaded piece on the decorative paper and then on the black card. Dab a tiny amount of tacky glue under the center of the wooden skewer to hold it in place.

CELESTIAL WIRE
By Phyllis Nelson

Cardstock: white, light blue
Metallic wrapping paper or cardstock in purple, turquoise & silver
Star & moon rubber stamp by Paula Best
Embossing pad & silver embossing powder
22-gauge silver wire
Self adhesive rhinestones
Purple glitter gel pen
Brush markers: gray, light pink, turquoise
Foam mounting tape

Directions: Stamp and emboss the star image with silver embossing powder onto white cardstock. Color the star with purple glitter gel pen. Color the remaining parts of the image with brush markers as shown, shading moon face with gray and adding pink to the cheeks and lips. Cut out the star. Attach a large piece of foam mounting tape to the back. Cut metallic papers into three sizes of rectangles and layer on a light blue card. Leave a larger band of purple exposed. Attach the rhinestones to the wider side of the purple metallic paper. Using a length of silver wire, form a tail and spiral the end. Remove the protective cover of the foam tape and lay the tail onto it so that the tail flows down from the star. Attach the star to the top of the silver metallic paper.

MY SONS
By Sandi Allan

Cardstock
Patterned paper
Vellum
Wire
Jewel stars
Star die cut
Clear thread

Directions: Print a poem on light colored paper using a computer. Choose which words to highlight. Print just these words on colored vellum. Print names on colored vellum as well. Mat the names and journaling with a darker color. Layer all flat materials and adhere. Add stars, vellum die cuts, beads, and brads. Bend wire and attach by making small holes and threading clear thread through the back and tying.

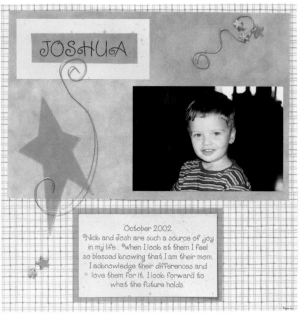

Dry Embossing: *To dry emboss words or images into paper, lay a stencil on the paper; attach with removable tape. Place face down over a light source (e.g., a window or light box). With an embossing stylus, trace around the cut-out portion of the stencil. The stencil image will be dimensionally represented on the paper's surface.*

YOSEMITE VALLEY
By Sandi Allan

Cardstock
Wire
Beads
Embellishments
Leaves
Square punches in two sizes
Bronze leaves by Scrapyard

Directions: Punch squares out of dark paper and cut in half diagonally. Glue these to the corners of some photos. To embellish tags, punch small holes in tags and add wire with beads. Curl ends of wires. Add smaller square punched cutouts, leaves, and embellishments to complement layout. Adhere all elements to pages.

Ribbon

Ribbons are a cinch! See how a colored ribbon simply wrapped around a photo or journaling mats draws the viewer's interest. A charming bow or braid adds a compelling accent to a simple card or layout.

VICTORIAN BEAUTY
By Marian Wilde

Soft metallic gold cardstock by Golden Oak
Stamp by Paper Inspirations
Gold Brilliance inkpad
Vintage (or tea-dyed) lace
Mother-of-pearl buttons
Gold thread
Ribbon
Pink chalk

Directions: On gold cardstock, stamp the collage image using gold ink. Embellish the side of the card with lace, ribbon and mother-of-pearl buttons using tacky glue or a hot glue gun. Highlight the woman's cheeks and a few of the rose petals or buds with pink chalk.

ASIAN BEAUTY
By Janis Ramsden

Cardstock: black, green, white
Asian-lady stamp
Asian writing stamp by JudiKins
Black inkpad
Gold embossing powder
Embossing inkpad
Leaf patterned paper
Beads & three gold jewelry pins
Decorative ribbons or fabric

Directions: Using black ink, stamp the Asian lady image on white paper. Redden the lips with a marker. Cut out the image. Emboss the Asian writing image in gold on dark green paper. Cut a mat of leaf patterned paper slightly smaller than the black card you plan to use for your base card. Inside dimensions should be large enough to frame the lady. Cut a white then a black piece of cardstock to border the inside of the mat opening as shown. The smallest opening will be the black mat. Glue the three mats together. Slip coordinating beads on two separate gold metal jewelry pins. Attach these pins to a third jewelry pin and insert into the hair of the Asian woman. Adhere to the back of the paper with tape. Wrap ribbons around the shoulders of the lady's image and glue in place. Glue the solid green background piece to your black card. Using double-sided tape, attach lady onto this background. Frame the piece with the triple mat using more double-sided tape.

SPRING BRAID (DETAIL)
By Debby DeBenedetti

Cardstock
Ribbons
Charms

A pretty ribbon braid decorates the edge of this page. The ribbon is attached at each end with extra ribbon threaded through holes punched in the cardstock. Gold charms add the finishing touch.

VICTORIAN SHOE
By Marian Wilde

Cardstock: natural parchment, cream
Stamps by Stamp Francisco
Lace & ribbon
Buttons
Gold Brilliance inkpad
Spray adhesive

Directions: On a natural parchment card, stamp a lacy image as a background in metallic gold ink. Some unstamped space should be left on the card to provide contrast. Using spray adhesive, attach a piece of lace cut the same size as the front of the card. Glue a narrow nylon ribbon to the edge of the card on the right side. Using cream cardstock, stamp the shoe image in the same gold ink and cut out. Mount the shoe on top of the lace using foam mounting tape. Add satin bow and button embellishments.

EASTER GREETINGS
By Jennifer Gaub

Colored cardstock
Basket punch by Punch Bunch
Black inkpad
Egg punch by EK Success
"Happy Easter" rubber stamp
Foam mounting tape

Directions: Stamp greeting on colored paper. Cut out and adhere to folded card. Glue punched eggs to card and add basket with foam tape for dimension. Add a small bow to complete the look.

FRIENDS (DETAILS)
By Debby DeBenedetti

Cardstock
Ribbons
Purchased tag

Simply wrapping brightly colored ribbons around photo or journaling mats draws interest and also adds dimension and color to a summer scene.

FLORAL WITH BOW
By Jaye Green

Cardstock: white, lavender, purple
Patterned paper
Stamp by Penny Black
Black inkpad & embossing powder
Patterned paper
Watercolor markers
Ribbon
Foam mounting tape

Directions: Stamp the flower image in black on white paper and emboss. Color with watercolor markers. Cut out the design with scissors or a craft knife. Use foam mounting tape to adhere layers. Finish with a ribbon bow.

BLUE BALLERINA
By Krista Camacho

Cardstock
Stamp by Impression Obsession
Royal blue pigment inkpad
Galaxy embossing powder by JudiKins
Blue tulle
Craft knife

Directions: Cut and fold base card. Cut light blue square and a smaller dark blue square. Stamp image on small square and emboss. Cut slit in image where bodice meets the skirt, using a craft knife. Place tulle in slit and adhere using double-sided tape. Trim bottom of skirt along hemline. Assemble layers of card and adhere.

Fibers & Raffia

Fibers, like ribbon, add a soft dimension to paper. Whether soft and supple, or coarse, they can set the tone of the page, defining it as elegant or down-home. Consider metallic thread, raffia, cording, yarn, or whatever sparks your creativity.

SIMPLE THINGS BOOKMARK
By Janis Ramsden

Cardstock: gold, burgundy
Stamp by Hero Arts
Hole punch
Yarns, ribbon, thread, & charms

Directions: Stamp saying on burgundy cardstock and emboss with gold powder. Attach to gold paper. Punch hole at top and tie with fibers and charms.

BUILDING TRUST
By Jennifer Gaub

Cardstock
Patterned paper
Alphabet template
Vellum tag & heart mesh eyelet by Making Memories
Brads
Eyelets & eyelet tools
Fibers

Directions: Cut title out of patterned paper using large alphabet template. Layer elements and add fibers with white brads. Attach tag and eyelets and adhere.

TAKE TIME TO SMELL THE FLOWERS
By Sandi Allan

Cardstock
Patterned paper
Square, daisy, & dragonfly punches
Colored raffia
Mulberry paper
Wave template
Gel pen

Directions: Mat photos with complementary mulberry papers. Wet the borders of the mulberry paper with water and pull apart to create fuzzy edge. Trace wave pattern using template and cut out. Layer papers and photos and add raffia on edges, securing on the back with tape. Punch out squares, daisies, and dragonflies and stack to match layout. Cut wings from some of the dragonflies and attach to whole dragonflies for a dimensional look. Draw dashed flying line using a gel pen.

BE MY LOVE (DETAIL)
By Debby DeBenedetti

Cardstock
Patterned paper
Corrugated paper
Letter stamps
Circle punch
Fibers
Buttons
Glass micro beads

Directions: Tear, cut, and secure a variety of papers together for the border. Wrap fibers around the border piece, stringing stamped and punched circles as you go. Adhere to the background cardstock. Adorn tag using assorted fibers and glass micro beads glued to the bottom torn edge. Add buttons.

TALL OAKS FROM LITTLE ACORNS GROW
By Sandi Allan

Cardstock
Patterned paper
Mulberry paper
Raffia
Leaves
Miscellaneous embellishments & mementos

Directions: Use torn paper to make photo mats. Punch holes and thread with raffia. Use mulberry paper to make a frame within a frame. Adhere all mats and photos, then attach leaves and other embellishments.

Natural & Organic

Nature's materials, whether collected by hand on a pleasant outdoor excursion or purchased at your local store, add color and texture to your pages. Even simple twigs and leaves will warm up a page design.

BIRDHOUSE
By Phyllis Nelson

Cardstock: cream, rust, green, brown
Birdhouse stamp by Rubber Stampede
Watercolor brush markers
Raffia or rope
Twigs

Directions: Use watercolor markers to color the image on the rubber stamp. Stamp the image on cream cardstock. Cut around the stamped piece and glue it to green paper. Layer on rust paper and then on a brown card. Threads may be pulled from a piece of raffia or natural fiber rope to tie the twigs together. Using glue, affix twigs on the side of the stamped image.

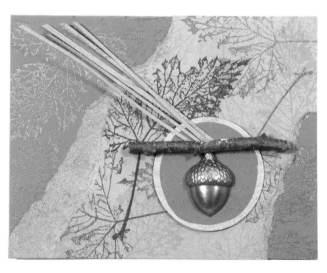

FATHER AND SON OUTING
By Debby DeBenedetti

Cardstock
Vellum
Skeleton leaves
Eyelets & eyelet tools
String

Directions: Create manila envelope-style photo mats by scoring and folding cardstock to overlap photos at the top and bottom. Punch circles from dark cardstock and attach with eyelets. Add thin string around closures. Make leaf holder with vellum and eyelets.

ACORN
By Janis Ramsden

Cardstock: rust, kraft, metallic gold
Skeleton leaf stamp by Fred Mullet
Metallic Rub-Ons
Inkpads: gold, purple, butterscotch
Acorn charm
Twig

Directions: Using purple and butterscotch inkpads, stamp kraft-colored paper with the leaf stamp. Tear off corners as shown. Stamp leaf in gold ink on rust paper. Cut a circle of metallic gold cardstock and a slightly smaller circle of rust paper. Layer papers as shown and adhere to card. Cut five narrow strips of kraft paper. Attach acorn charm, twig, and thin strips of paper with tacky glue.

PRIMITIVE FIGURES
By Phyllis Nelson

Tan cardstock
Dark brown handmade paper with texture
Stamp by Personal Stamp Exchange
Colored pencils or chalks
Black inkpad
Natural wooden & black beads
Thin black cord
Needle & thread

Directions: Stamp figures twice with black ink on tan cardstock. Cut out one set of figures. From the second set, cut out the figure on the left and tape it to the right of the group of four. To color, lightly pencil or chalk using earth tones. Sew beads as shown. Using tacky glue, adhere a flat bead to the head of the second figure. With a small brush, wet the dark brown paper where it is to be torn. Tear and attach to the card using black cord. Knot the cord at the bottom of the card, leaving the ends free. Place double-sided tape on the back of the stamped image, covering the areas where the buttons were sewn. Glue figures to the card.

PRESERVING NATURE: Purchased skeleton leaves and pressed flowers are elegant, but you can also create your own accents. No fancy flower presses are needed, just tuck fresh cuttings of leaves and flowers into an old phone book for a week or two. Other items collected in your travels, such as a feather, twig or bit of straw can be preserved, too. Just seal in plastic bags and freeze for several weeks to eliminate any organisms that may be lurking.

HARVEST MOON
By Linda Lavasani

Black cardstock
Large bamboo stamp by Beeswax
Black embossing powder & pigment ink
Bleach
Cotton swabs
Radiant Pearls: Fandango Green, Tiger Eye, Bitter Apple, & Brass Rail
Spray fixative

Directions: Stamp the bamboo on black cardstock using black pigment ink and emboss using black powder. Apply bleach sparingly to the paper using a cotton swab, brushing in the same direction with diagonal strokes. Vary the pressure and length of the strokes to achieve a mottled effect. Allow bleached paper to dry. Paint the image using Tiger Eye, Fandango Green and Brass Rail for the bamboo stalks and Bitter Apple and Fandango Green for the bamboo leaves. When dry, seal with a spray fixative. Cut out the stamped medallion and adhere to project.

Flowers

E xquisite one-of-a-kind cards created by Phyllis Nelson showcase beautiful pressed flowers and leaves. Press your own floral souvenirs between the pages of an old book for a few weeks, then incorporate them in your designs.

PETAL AND LEAF MOSAICS
By Phyllis Nelson

Pressed leaves & flower petals
Sticker paper
Gold embossing powder
Gold pen
Gold metallic paper for background
Colored layering papers to match leaves or petals
Matte finish Mod Podge

Directions: Cut a basic shape from sticker paper. Peel the backing from one side. Place whole pressed flowers, leaves or petals on the sticky part of the paper. Add extra leaves or petals to the blank areas in contrasting colors. After the larger white spaces of the adhesive sheet are covered, use broken pieces of foliage to fill as much space as possible. This is important since large areas of embossing powder may crack. Allow the foliage to extend over the edges of the sticker paper to assure complete coverage. Then trim. Dust the entire piece with embossing powder. It is not necessary to worry about static as the extra embossing powder adds to the effect. Place the decorated shape on a heat-resistant surface and hold it down with a wooden skewer while embossing. Hold the heat tool several inches above the surface, moving it immediately when the powder melts. Apply tiny amounts of tacky glue to any petal that becomes loose during the heating process. Touch up any unembossed areas with a gold Krylon pen. Coat with a thin layer of matte finish Mod Podge. Layer as shown. A thin edge of gold metallic paper frames the shape and complements the gold embossing.

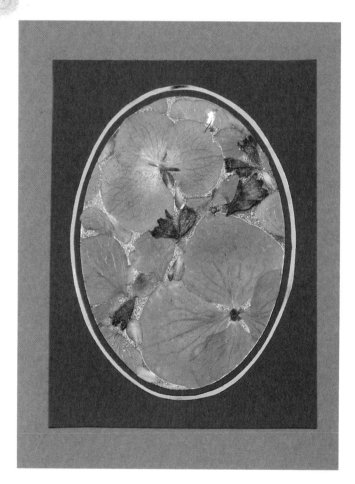

HYDRANGEA OVAL

The central flowers are lavender hydrangea florets. (One hydrangea blossom consists of many florets. They press nicely and keep their beautiful color.) The open space is filled with petal pieces of blue hydrangea, coral bells and pink miniature rose petals. A blue-violet border highlights the color of the petals.

AUTUMN LEAVES

A trio of bright fall leaves establish the color theme of this card. A collection of yellow rose petal pieces makes a subtle background and complements the autumnal motif.

CORAL BELLS

The central focal point is a stem of coral bells. Tiny blue lobelia and violas fill out the floral spray. The remaining space is filled in with broken pieces of leaves, creating the "mosaic" portion of the card.

LAVENDER AND YELLOW

A hydrangea floret is surrounded by little violas. The purple and lavender-colored flowers float in a sea of yellow buttercup petals. A blue-violet border frames the flowers.

PANSIES

A large pansy anchors the collage. Smaller violas also add to the bouquet. Pieces of petals of other pink, purple, and lavender flowers complete the composition.

Layering

Cards make the ultimate personal gift for your loved ones. The distinctive cards pictured here display the effects you can create by layering, punching, and paper folding courtesy of Stamper's Warehouse's talented designers.

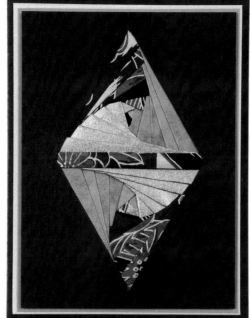

IRIS FOLDED ASIAN PEAR
By Kathy Yee

Cardstock: rust, gold
Four coordinating patterned papers (Washi, mulberry, wrapping, & gold)
Pear stamp by The Artful Stamper
Word stamp
Gold metallic inkpad
Egyptian Gold embossing powder by JudiKins
Foam mounting tape
Book: *Iris Folding for the Winter* by Maruscha Gaasenbeek & Tine Beauveser (Forte Publishers)

Directions: Stamp rust colored card with pear stamp twice and emboss with gold ink. Stamp and emboss words in gold and emboss. Cut center from one pear image. Use instructions and pattern with four papers instead of three from *Iris Folding for the Winter* book. Tape papers to cover entire hole. Add completed pear to layered card with foam mounting tape.

IRIS FOLDING DIAMOND
By Kathy Yee

Cardstock: dark green, medium green
Coordinating patterned papers
Gold paper
Gold leafing pen by Krylon
Removable tape
Foam mounting tape
Book: *Iris Folding with Envelopes* by Maruscha Gaasenbeek & Tine Beauveser (Forte Publishers)

Directions: Adhere the medium green cardstock to the dark green card with double-sided tape. Outline the medium green cardstock with the gold leafing pen. Cut out the diamond using the diamond pattern from the *Iris Folding with Envelopes* book. Lay the green cardstock with the diamond cutout face down over the diamond paper pattern using removable tape to hold it in place. Using the instructions from book, cut strips of each of the three papers and fold in half lengthwise. Identify each type paper as A, B, & C. Fold one strip of paper in thirds and lay across the center of the diamond. Use tape to hold in place. Lay the strips of paper as indicated on the pattern of the top triangle with the folded edge of the paper against the pattern lines. Hold each paper in place with a small piece of removable tape. Alternate papers A, B, and C around the pattern. Repeat the process for the triangle on the bottom, then remove the card from the pattern. Fill the final holes (Iris) with any one of the three papers (unfolded). Cover all of the strips completely with the adhesive tape and adhere to card with foam mounting tape.

CHEVRON CARD
By Diana Diaz

Cardstock: black, rust, moss
Patterned papers
Chevron punch
Grape appliqué

Directions: Cut and fold back cardstock to 5¼" square. Cut rust background paper to 5" square. Punch 12 chevrons, four from each of three coordinating papers. Adhere one green-patterned chevron in each corner of the rust square. Glue a moss chevron below each green-patterned chevron. Glue one black patterned chevron in each of the four rust triangles which have now been formed. Cut a center square of black 2⅛" square and adhere with grape appliqué.

FLORAL PUNCHED RED ROSES
By Kathy Yee

Cardstock: white, red, gold
Words stamp by A Stamp in the Hand
Metallic gold inkpad
Cat's Eyes in Hunter Green, Moss Green & Scarlet
     by Colorbox
Small & medium flower punches
3-flower corner punch
Leaf punches in 3 sizes
3-D Paper Tole Tool & Pad
Pointed craft tweezers
Embossing stylus with large tip
Gold leafing pen by Krylon

Directions: Punch out enough petals to make two
flowers and one bud. Curl the petals by placing the
punched flower piece on the molding pad. With
the rounded end of the 3-D Paper Tole Tool or the
large end of the stylus, hold the tool at right
angles to the pad and press down firmly moving
from the outer edge to the center of the flower to
give dimension to the piece. Layer the punched
petals to form the flowers. Glue with tacky glue.
Offset each layer. Repeat to form the bud. Stamp
the leaves by applying ink from the Cat's Eyes
directly to the stamp, using several colors for a
shaded effect. Stamp two leaves directly on the
white cardstock. Attach the roses and bud to this
piece. Punch out the different sized leaves after
they are stamped and curl them. Stamp words several times with gold ink on the base card and layer
cardstock pieces with adhesive. Arrange the flowers on the white cardstock and adhere. Dip the
corners of the leaves in glue and tuck in behind
and around the flowers. Run the gold leafing pen
over some of the flower edges. Layer paper as
shown and mount on card stamped with word
stamp in metallic gold ink.

FLORAL PUNCHED ZINNIAS
By Kathy Yee

Cardstock: white, silver, pale pink
Vellum: white, silver
Silver decorative paper
Background stamp by JudiKins
Metallic silver inkpad
Punches: small & medium sunflower, tiny sun,
     medium & large leaf
Paper crimper
Diamond Dots stickers by Stampendous
3-D Paper Tole Tool & Pad
Embossing stylus with large tip

Directions: Crimp pink rectangle with paper
crimper. cut a rectangle of blue paper slightly larger
than pink rectangle. Stamp card with background
stamp in metallic silver. Follow the directions for the
Floral Punched Red Roses (left) using sunflower
stamps and silver papers to create a zinnia themed
card. Add a diamond dot sticker to the center of
each flower for interest.

BLUE JEANS
By Diana Diaz

Cardstock: red, white
Ultramarine inkpad by Fabrico
Heart punches
Heart eyelets and eyelet tools
Jeans stamp by JudiKins

Directions: Generously apply ultramarine ink to
jeans stamp. Set stamp down, rubber side up. Place
folded white card over stamp. Apply pressure and
carefully lift off paper. Re-ink pocket area only and
apply small piece of cardstock over pocket area.
Apply pressure and lift off. Cut out. Punch out red
hearts and layer with pocket piece. Use heart eyelets
on pocket.

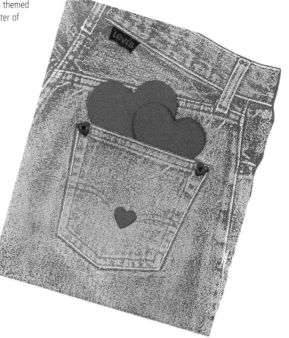

Photography

What image is more endearing than a family photo? Select black-and-white photos from your personal collection to hand-color and highlight with distinctive framing. Stamping on photos creates a variety of effects. If you're hesitant to alter an original photo, make a colored photocopy.

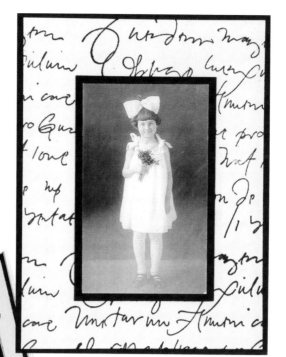

PHOTO CARDS
By Sue Astroth

Black cardstock
Cream cardstock stamped with your favorite background/script stamp
Gold leafing pen
Ready-made cards & envelopes in black or cream
Color copies of your favorite photos, resized as necessary to fit card size
Pages from old book, such as an encyclopedia or shorthand guide.

Directions: Trim the copies of your photos and layer with black cardstock so small border of the black shows around the photo. Cut your background (either the book page or your stamped cream cardstock) to fit the card you are using. Layer as shown in photo. Use a gold leafing pen to highlight the edges of the black cardstock for just a little sparkle.

STAMPING OF PHOTOS
By Terrece Siddoway

Black stamp pad – Memories, Archival, Ancient Page or Staz-On work best

Directions: Here's a great way to reuse all those extra photos that aren't first-rate. Making them into greeting cards yields dramatic results. Ink stamp in black and stamp on the photo background. Be careful as the stamp may slip on the photo's glossy surface. Let dry for five minutes. Areas that aren't completely covered can be filled in with a permanent marker.

BLACK AND WHITE PHOTO COLORIZATION
By Terrece Siddoway

SpotPen system used for all samples

Directions: Colorizing black and white photos makes them come alive and coordinate with colors of your page layouts. The SpotPen system works great on almost all paper surfaces and takes only minutes compared to conventional hand coloring. The dye is Ph Neutral and as lightfast as any retouching dye. Even copy paper looks good with this system. Coloring only the main subjects directs the eye to the focal point..

The kitten and the girl were printed on heavy glossy paper. The boys were printed on soft glossy paper. The photos of the boy on horse were printed on textured mat paper. The top photo is tinted by computer; the second photo has only the subjects tinted by hand, with the background left in black and white as contrast.

CROPPING: Artful and close cropping on most photos makes for more dramatic layouts. Decide whether the background enhances or detracts from the subject. Scanning photos and other memorabilia gives you greater control and more freedom to explore page layouts. Use purchased or hand-cut mats or layer on contrasting papers to create exciting borders for your photos.

Boxes

Small boxes have undeniable appeal, and these clever containers are real showstoppers with their lively patterns, colors, and shapes. A box always holds surprises and these are no exception.

MUSIC BOX
By Sue Astroth

Small Jewelry box
Vintage sheet music
Cardstock: cream, black
Inkpads: black, copper, sepia, rust
Stipple brush
Stamp for box top image
Found letters & game pieces
Sewing snaps
Small alphabet stamps

Directions: Cover the jewelry box with vintage sheet music. Stamp main image with black ink on cream paper and tear around it. Glue the watch face, stamped images, snap and found letters to the box top. Glue 24 snaps around the edge of the box lid. Let dry. Using alphabet stamps, stamp the letters for the message that goes inside the box in sepia or black on off-white cardstock. Cut out the letters. Following photo, glue stamped letters and game pieces with tacky glue to inside of box.

DREAM BOX
By Sue Astroth

3^{1}/$_{2}$" square jewelry box
Washi paper
Cardstock: white, blue
Cloud stamp & background stamp
Blue inkpad
Stipple brush
Alphabet stamps
^{3}/$_{4}$ sheer ribbon, 24" long
Wooden beads for box feet
Assorted beads for decoration
Gold pen by Krylon

Directions: Cover a 3^{1}/$_{2}$" x 3^{1}/$_{2}$" jewelry box with washi paper. Stamp sheets of white cardstock with cloud stamp in blue ink. Stipple blue ink around clouds to tint the white paper. Cut into 3" x 3" squares. Stamp letters to spell out "dream" on the squares Cut six 3^{1}/$_{4}$" x 3^{1}/$_{4}$" squares from solid blue cardstock. Lay the sheer ribbon on work surface. Starting 6" from one end of the ribbon, evenly space "dream" on the ribbon and glue in place. Punch a hole in the center of the remaining square of blue cardstock. Bring the top edge of the ribbon through and tie a small knot. Glue the square to the inside of the box top, hiding the knot. For feet, glue four wooden beads to the bottom of the box. To decorate the top of box, cut a 2^{1}/$_{2}$" x 2^{1}/$_{2}$" square of blue cardstock. Edge with gold pen and set aside to dry. Stamp the background design on white cardstock and trim to 2^{1}/$_{4}$" x 2^{1}/$_{4}$". Center this on top of the blue cardstock and place both on the center of the box top. Following the photo, decorate the top of the box with assorted beads.

ARTIFACT BOX
By Lari Drendell

Cardstock
Cream-colored polymer clay
Rubber stamps
Small matchbox
Burnt umber & sienna acrylic paints
Sienna acrylic paint
Gold paint
Decorative papers
Black inkpad

Directions: After conditioning polymer clay, make a pendant shape, about ^{1}/$_{4}$" thick, for the top of the box. Imprint the clay with a script or decorative uninked rubber stamp. Shape sides and round corners of the clay to fit onto the matchbox top. Bake for 20 minutes at 265°F. Let cool. Add antiquing lines, cracks and pits with a craft knife. Highlight these marks by rubbing with burnt umber paint. Continue to rub until paint dries. Wait for a few minutes then rub gently with a damp paper towel to remove excess paint. Cover the outside of the box with decorative paper. Wrap around edges and glue. Attach baked piece to the top of the box with tacky glue. Paint drawer of matchbox inside and out with gold paint. Roll polymer clay to approximately ^{1}/$_{16}$" thick and cut into five pieces. All pieces should fit inside the box. Stamp impressions with black ink on one side of each piece and bake as above. Cut a piece of cardstock 6^{1}/$_{2}$" x 1^{7}/$_{8}$". Sponge both sides of paper with burnt umber and sienna paint. Accordion fold the cardstock into five equal sections. Attach clay tiles to the paper with double stick tape. Tape the first section of the tiles into the bottom of the box. Fold the remaining pieces inside the box bottom.

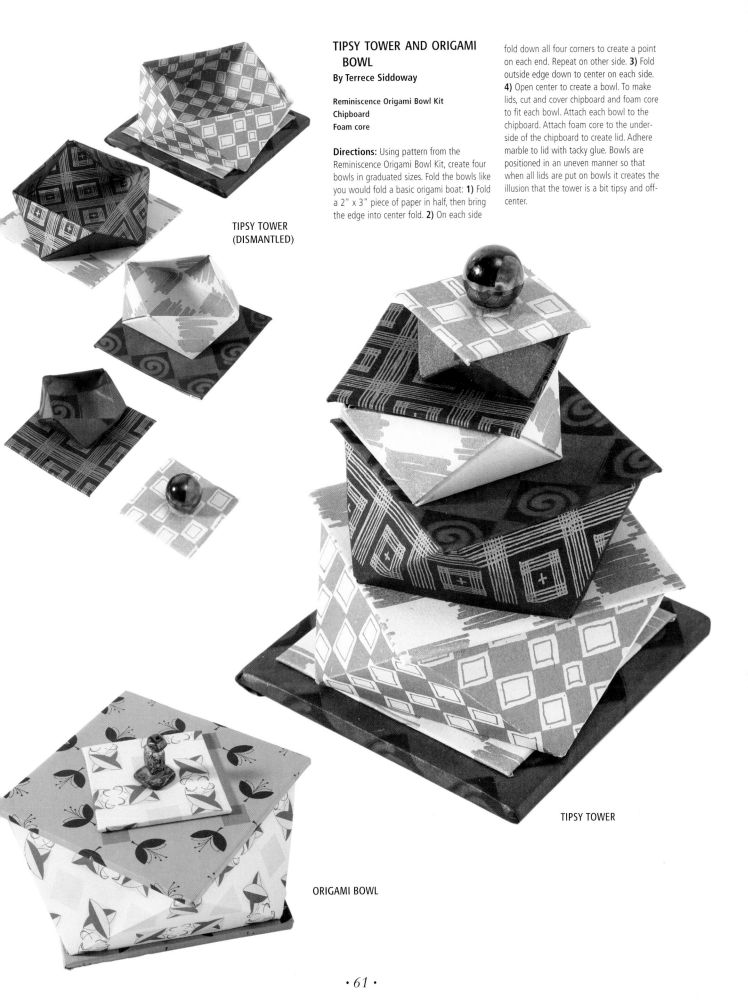

TIPSY TOWER AND ORIGAMI BOWL

By Terrece Siddoway

Reminiscence Origami Bowl Kit
Chipboard
Foam core

Directions: Using pattern from the Reminiscence Origami Bowl Kit, create four bowls in graduated sizes. Fold the bowls like you would fold a basic origami boat: **1)** Fold a 2" x 3" piece of paper in half, then bring the edge into center fold. **2)** On each side fold down all four corners to create a point on each end. Repeat on other side. **3)** Fold outside edge down to center on each side. **4)** Open center to create a bowl. To make lids, cut and cover chipboard and foam core to fit each bowl. Attach each bowl to the chipboard. Attach foam core to the underside of the chipboard to create lid. Adhere marble to lid with tacky glue. Bowls are positioned in an uneven manner so that when all lids are put on bowls it creates the illusion that the tower is a bit tipsy and off-center.

TIPSY TOWER
(DISMANTLED)

TIPSY TOWER

ORIGAMI BOWL

The Designers

SANDI ALLAN
Originally from South Africa, Sandi is an interior designer and scrap-book artist. She has been scrap-booking for 4 years. Her hobbies include gardening, sewing, and music. Sandi uses her two boys and travel for her inspired designs.

KRISTA CAMACHO
In 2001, Krista joined the creative team at Stamper's Warehouse where her expertise has flourished. She has been stamping and scrapbooking for 9 years. Drawn to art and the creative process, she especially enjoys working on projects which reveal their own direction and themes during their creation.

SUE ASTROTH
Sue, a native Californian, has been stamping and quilting for 20 years. A few years after her move to the Bay Area from Southern California, she joined the Stamper's Warehouse team. Her first book, *Fast and Easy Scrapbook Quilts*, was released in February 2004.

VANESSA COLE
Vanessa is a former elementary school teacher who is part of the Stamper's Warehouse staff. She has been a rubber stamper for 14 years and a scrapbooker for six years. Vanessa is an avid scrapbooker and book artist who also enjoys fast cars and music. She is passionate about her art and has an ability to translate her emotions into her scrapbook pages.

TRACI BAUTISTA
A California mixed media artist, art educator and graphic designer, Traci believes that there is an "artist" in everyone. She is an artist-in-resi-dence at the Palo Alto Art Center and also teaches workshops at paper art stores in California. Traci sells her unique hand-painted papers and one-of-a-kind aRt! kits for art jour-naling and stamping.

DEBBY DeBENEDETTI
Since 1998, Debby has enjoyed the creative challenges scrapbooking offers. She enjoys teaching tech-niques that stretch her abilities as well as those of her students. She is married and has two sons, Anthony and Cade.

PATTY CARLSON
Patty has been a rubber stamper and paper crafter for 10 years. She loves the way stamping has evolved as an art form and especially enjoys mak-ing pieces with Asian themes. Despite her demanding, full-time job, Patty indulges in her rubber stamp "addiction" almost every day. Her beautiful creations attest to her love and dedication.

BARBARA DeLAP
Barbara is well-known for her bookbinding and jewelry design classes. Her classes are always brimming with students eager to learn new and unique techniques. With her innovative sense of style, Barbara is a true original. Barbara wishes to acknowledge Pam Sussman and Gayle Burkins for their talent and inspiration in her bookbinding journey.

ADDITIONAL DESIGNS BY:
Lari Drendell, Emily Foytlin, Susan Gin, Jaye Green, DeAnne Velasco Musiel, April Nelson, Margaret Rodgers, and Marian Wilde

DIANA DIAZ

After 13 years of teaching rubber stamp classes, Diana is still going strong. She has been associated with Stamper's Warehouse from its beginning. Because of Diana's enthusiasm, many of her tennis students have found their way to rubber stamping. Diana's cards showcase the amazing possibilities of stamping techniques.

PHYLLIS NELSON

Phyllis, the creative force behind Stamper's Warehouse, enjoys sharing her love of stamping with her talented staff and customers. Her extensive experience with stamping and card-making is witnessed in her elegant style and versatile techniques.

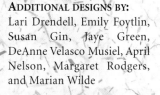

JENNIFER GAUB

Jenn is a true force of nature at Stamper's Warehouse and a leader of the Friday "Scrapping the Night Away" evenings. She puts the "art" in party and her expertise shows up in her great designs. Scrapping is a family affair for Jenn as evidenced in the layouts and photos of her two boys.

JANIS RAMSDEN

Janis was introduced to stamping many years ago by a good friend. She loves challenging herself artistically and learning new techniques through publications, classes, and her many stamping friends. A proficient stamper, her style is classic and refined.

LINDA LAVASANI

Linda's background has been in the banking and lending industry. She didn't discover her hidden artistic talents until she began rubber stamping in 1995. That is still her first love. She also enjoys refinishing furniture, designing polymer clay and beaded jewelry, and creating collage pieces.

TERRECE SIDDOWAY

Born in Idaho, Terrece graduated from Brigham Young University. She began stamping ten years ago. In addition to her job as store manager at Stamper's Warehouse, she teaches many popular classes in stamping and scrapbooking. Terrece's love of all things western is reflected in her projects. Her dog, Angel, assists in all of her creations.

SANDI MARR

A resident of Redwood City, California, Sandi has been stamping for 12 years. She is an enthusiastic teacher at Stamper's Warehouse and also makes samples for several rubber stamp companies. She stamps to pen pals, and enjoys book-making and mixed media art. Her beautifully detailed fabrications span a wide variety of applications and themes.

KATHY YEE

Kathy is a program manager for a semiconductor equipment company who enjoys stamping as a hobby. She was introduced to stamping by her old college roommate seven years ago and hasn't stopped since. Kathy enjoys stamping because it combines structure and creativity. She's been teaching for three years and her specialty is Asian designs.

Resources

Many of the products used in this book are available at your local craft and/or scrapbook retailer. Products may also be purchased through Stamper's Warehouse. For assistance in locating a retailer in your area, consult the companies below.

Note: Some of the stamped images and papers shown may no longer be available from the manufacturers. Stamps and papers from other companies may be used to achieve the same effects.

STAMPER'S WAREHOUSE
101-G Town & Country Dr.
Danville, CA 94526
925-362-9595; fax 925-362-0999
www.stamperswarehouse.com

ANGELWINGS – *Radiant Pearls*
3322 W. Sussex Way
Fresno, CA 93722
866-229-1544
www.radiantpearls.com

CLEARSNAP, INC. – *ColorBox inkpads, embossing pads*
P.O. Box 98
Anacortes, WA 98221
800-448-4862
www.clearsnap.com

CRAFT T PRODUCTS – *chalks, Rub-Ons*
P.O. Box 83
Fairmont, MN 56031
507-235-3996
www.craf-t-products.com

EK SUCCESS – *punches, stamps, markers, cutting tools*
125 Entin Rd.
Clifton, NJ 07014
973-458-0092
www.eksuccess.com

FISKARS MFG. CORP. – *paper crimper, decorative scissors, cutting tools*
7811 Stewart Ave.
Wausau, WI 54401-9071
715-842-2091
www.fiskars.com

GEMÉ ART INC. – *paper tole supplies*
209 W. 6th St.
Vancouver, WA 98660
800-426-4424
www.gemeart.com

GOLDEN ARTISTS COLORS, INC. – *glazes, acrylic paints, artist mediums*
188 Bell Road
New Berlin, NY 13411
607-847-6154
www.goldenpaints.com

JACQUARD – *Lumiere, Neopaque, textile paint, Pearl-Ex*
Rupert Gibbon & Spider
P.O. Box 425
Healdsburg, CA 95448
707-433-9577
www.jacquardproducts.com

JUDIKINS – *Diamond Glaze, Amazing Glaze, stamps*
17803 S. Harvard Blvd.
Gardena, CA 90248
310-515-1115
www.judikins.com

KRYLON – *metallic leafing pens, spray adhesive, spray fixatives*
101 Prospect Ave. NW
Cleveland, OH 44115
216-515-7693
www.krylon.com

LEISURE ARTS, INC. – *paper, books*
5701 Ranch Drive
Little Rock, AR 72223
800-643-8030
www.leisurearts.com

LINECO, INC. – *bookbinding supplies*
P.O. Box 1624
Holyoke, MA 04041
800-322-7775

MARVY UCHIDA – *Liquid Appliqué, cutting mats, punches, pens, heat tools*
3535 Del Amo Blvd.
Torrance, CA 90503
800-541-5877
www.uchida.com

POLYFORM PRODUCTS CO. – *Premo polymer clay, molds, Sculpey glaze*
1901 Estes Ave.
Elk Grove Village, IL 60007
847-427-0020
www.sculpey.com

RANGER INDUSTRIES, INC. – *Adirondack inkpads, Melting Pot, UTEE, craft sheets, Perfect Pearls, Nick Bantock inkpads*
15 Park Rd.
Tinton Falls, NJ 07724
908-389-3535

REMINISCENCE PAPERS – *Origami Bowl Kit*
2607 SW Custer St.
Portland, OR 97219
503-246-9681
www.reminiscencepapers.com

RUBBA DUB DUB – *hot glue, molds, fibers, embellishments, stamps*
800-763-2766
www.artsanctum.com

SPOT PEN – *photo colorization system*
Route 1 Box 97
Orlando, OK 73073
580-864-7753
www.spotpen.com

TOMBOW – *pens, glues*
800-835-3232
www.tombowusa.com

TSUKINEKO – *Brilliance inkpads, Fabrico inkpads, StazOn inkpads*
17640 NE 65th St.
Redmond, WA 98052-4904
800-769-6633
www.tsukineko.com

XYRON – *machines and refills for applying adhesive*
15820 N. 84th St.
Scottsdale, AZ 85260
800-793-3523
www.xyron.com

BOOK RESOURCES:
Greeting Card Magic with Rubber Stamps
By MaryJo McGraw
North Light Books, 4700 E. Galbraith Rd.
Cincinnati, OH 45236
513-531-2690

Iris Folding For the Winter
By Maruscha Gaasenbeek & Tine Beauveser
Forte Uitgevers Publishers, UK

Iris Folding with Envelopes
By Maruscha Gaasenbeek &
Tine Beauveser
Forte Uitgevers Publishers, UK

Volume II Non-Adhesive Binding: 1-2-& 3-Section Sewings
By Keith Smith
Keith Smith Publisher
1115 East Main St., Ste 219, Box 8
Rochester, NY 14609
585-482-2496
keith@keithsmithbooks.com

Volume III Non-Adhesive Binding: Exposed Spine Sewings
By Keith Smith
Keith Smith Publisher
(see above)